AUTUMN REFLECTIONS

AUTUMN REFLECTIONS

Enjoy!

Paul Krebill
2019

Paul Krebill

ISBN: Softcover 978-1-7960-4921-3
eBook 978-1-7960-4922-0

Print information available on the last page.

Rev. date: 08/01/2019

To order additional copies of this book, contact:
Xlibris
1-888-795-4274
www.Xlibris.com
Orders@Xlibris.com
793892

CONTENTS

BOOK II

Autobiographical Facts, Impressions And Memories

PREFACE

What one thinks is what one really is.
Proverbs 23:7

Autumn Reflections: *The lengthening shadows of autumn cast a spell of gentle reverie. In the final months of the year the dwindling of days causes one to ponder ones life and times, a pondering which can last the year round.*

Like the golden and scarlet leaves of Autumn, set free to drift toward the earth, one's thoughts and feelings, impressions and memories turn to beautiful hues of gold and red, mauve and rust, as they are carried on the wings of the autumn wind to the earth beneath. There to be collected as a testimony to the passing years of one's life.

INTRODUCTION

I am under no illusion that my own autumn reflections might attract great swarms of readers. But I do believe that those friends and family who want to know me better, will discover some clue in these pages. To that end what one finds here has not been written for some desired effect, but rather as an attempt to share my thoughts and reflections as honestly as possible with whomever might be interested.

Book I then, begins with written recording of random thoughts about the current scene as well as past events and experiences. A blend of thought and feeling, in an attempt to reveal honestly my own thoughts and reactions to events and developments.

Some of these essays are my deeply felt responses to serious issues of our time. Others are reflections, less profound, upon the current scene. Still other pages contain more light-hearted thoughts. I've called these *WRY BREAD.....Food for thought with a wry twist.*

Also shared here are musings of a more personal nature somewhat like journal entries from time to time. Book I need not be read all at once but from time to time as the reader wishes.

In Book II is an autobiographical section with facts pertaining to my life and some of my own memories and feelings about my life, as well as genealogical information pertaining to my family roots as well as that of my wife, Doris's family roots.

An appendix is included at the end which may be of interest to the reader.

PART 1

ESSAYS

–November.....2004

REFERENDUM
on the Morning after the2004 Election

The conservatives won by three million or so votes. More votes than the liberal cause could muster. Why? There was a lot of talk during the campaign about *REFERENDUM.* Some said that the campaign was a referendum on the incumbent president, George W. Bush. Others said it was a referendum on the leadership abilities and policies of the challenger, John Kerry. But, I believe on a much deeper level the 2004 election was a referendum on the 1960's, when both the God-given authority for personal behavior and the power and rightness of the United States were severely challenged. What had resulted forty years earlier was a strong anti-institutional mood along with the exaltation of personal freedom and individual self-expression. In that same period America was waging a seemingly endless war in Viet Nam. The authority and policies of our government were challenged by the anti-institutional and personal fulfillment liberal attitudes of the 1960's. A challenge to America's power was so strong that we were forced to flee Viet Nam as losers, and a great deal of our traditional moral consensus is integrated along with our pride as a nation.

These twin challenges to American values of personal purity and public power were more than half of today's voting population could stomach. So now, forty years later, the candidate who embodied the ignominy of our failure in Viet Nam by opposing the war in which he had fought, and the candidate who supported such issues of personal freedom as abortion rights and gays and lesbian rights went down in defeat. The candidate who touted a personal faith in God and espoused family values, and who had given us an opportunity to redeem ourselves militarily by going to war in the Middle East won the acceptance of a slight majority of Americans for whom the liberalism of the 1960's was an anathema.

I believe, however, that this was a misleading distinction fostered by the incumbent's campaign. By using the term "liberal" to sum up everything which many conservative Americans do not like about the so called cultural revolution of the 60's, and then by unfairly labeling the challenger a *liberal*, the challenger came to be seen as the embodiment of all that has been considered wrong with America since the 1960's. By contrast the incumbent was pictured as the one to bring American values back. Back to what they were in the good old days before the 1960's. This distinction served the incumbent's campaign well. Apparently for a little over half of those who voted there was comfort in what they believed was a vote to honor God and to affirm American power once again. They believe they have won a referendum on the cultural slide of the 60's.

–December2004

WHEN COLORED LIGHTS TWINKLE AND SNOW BEGINS TO SWIRL

What is it about this time of the year when it is dark by supper time and when colored lights twinkle along roof lines? What is it about December when thoughts turn to days gone by and it feels good to put on the sweater and woolen gloves again. It's a time to be home and to re-connect with one's extended family wherever they may be. It's an *"over the hills and through the woods to Grandmother's house we go"* time of the year.

Perhaps it is in our genes to begin to head toward home as winter approaches, to be enveloped in the warmth of an open fireplace and in the loving embrace of one's family. For our primal ancestors autumn was the time to return to the cave with its welcoming fire at the entrance, and to wrap up in blankets of fur for the annual winter survival. Typical scenes from the western frontier depict the lone rider huddled in his long coat with swirling snow whipping him as he approaches a tiny cabin, its solitary window brightly illuminated. It is early winter and it is evening, a gentle column of wood smoke is curling upward from the chimney. The cold and the dark would soon be upon him except for the warmth of home soon to surround him.

So with us now. We need to be with family, if at all possible, during this holiday time of year. "Will the kids be home for Christmas?" Or "Where do you plan to spend the holidays?" These questions are pleasant reminders of the season, friendly queries to which, hopefully, we can give a good answer. It's an *"I'll Be Home for Christmas"* time of the year.

So pack up the car, or put another leaf in the dining room table so that you can be together with loved ones and friends. Or if you can't, do make some phone calls. Don't let the frenzy of the season's rush take away the sweet anticipation of Santa and the tree, the joyful faces young and old, and the deep and inspiring spiritual thoughts which come to us as we contemplate the real meaning of the season.

WRY BREAD.....food for thought with a wry twist
–December 2004--some seasonal observations

GOODBYE CHRISTMAS?

It used to be that the most common expression heard in the last week of December was MERRY CHRISTMAS. So common that no one thought much about it. This year in 2004 that simple phrase of good will is under assault. A few years ago the season itself was under assault.

In those days there was an effort to put Christ back into Christmas. In the light of the fact that there is now an attempt to take Christ out of the season there is a question. Either they were wrong to assume that Christ had departed Christmas, or they were quite successful in putting him back in, for the current attackers believe that Christ is very much in Christmas, and so the eason MERRY CHRISTMAS must be purged in that it is a Christian expression and therefore to be banned from public use, lest it offend those of other religious persuasions, or more importantly, lest it anger those with no religious interest at all.

The promoters of putting Christ back into Christmas used to like the cute little phrase, *"HE (Jesus) is the reason for the season."* Certainly from a historical perspective they were right. The birth of Christ is in fact what the Christmas Season is all about. When Jesus is taken out of the season, there is a very real question as to what the reason for the season is. Perhaps it lies in the recommended alternative to MERRY CHRISTMAS, which is HAPPY HOLIDAYS. Common usage of this alternative suggests that the whole late December thing has to do with a holiday from whatever else has been going on in your life, especially work. Next thing we know the holiday won't be on December 25, but on the nearest Monday, as in the case of Lincoln's birthday.

However, the problem with HAPPY HOLIDAYS–as yet apparently undiscovered–is that *holiday* is a contraction of HOLY DAY, which in this case refers to the holy day on which Christ was born. Now it would appear that we are back to square one. Christ has a way of remaining firmly implanted both in Christmas and in this particular holiday time. He really is the reason for the season–rather than just to have an excuse to get off from work

So maybe it isn't Goodbye Christmas, after all. And, by the way, if the word *Christmas* goes, so must *Goodbye.* It is a contraction of GOD be with you.

–January 2005

"TIME'S UP, GOD'S KINGDOM IS HERE"

Reflections after reading Stanley Hauerwas, John Howard Yoder and Donald Kraybill

If we take seriously what Jesus actually did and how he related to people during the time he was with us historically, and if we believe that he calls us to follow him as his disciples, then we will begin to see how he wants us to act in society. He calls us to an alternative way of relating to other individuals and groups. The Gospels report that Jesus began his public ministry with the proclamation "The Kingdom of God has come near."(Mark1:15 NRSV) However else the kingdoms of this world act, Jesus comes presenting and embodying a new way, the way of God. His own life reveals the Kingdom of God into which he calls us. Therefore we must find the real Jesus in the real world as told to us in the Gospels.

When we turn to the Gospel stories with this expectancy we find a man whose radically new approach to others and to society so threatened and enraged those who followed the existing way, and were embedded in the prevailing power structures, that they killed him. Then when we take seriously Jesus' command to us to "take up our cross and follow him," we become uncomfortable thinking about what crosses may be ahead for us as well!

Over time Christians and the Church have tended to avoid the challenge of Jesus' call to an alternative way and what that might cost us. We avoid the cost of living according to Jesus' alternative way, by spiritualizing Jesus and deferring the Kingdom, rationalizing that Jesus and the Kingdom are not of this world, and that in this "knock down, rough and tumble" world we must make it through on our own terms acting as others do. We focus on Jesus as Divine Savior (not so much as Lord) and his saving us from our sins. We relegate the Kingdom of God to a heavenly state of affairs yet to come–beyond history.

To be sure the belief that Jesus' death on the cross in some mysterious divinely appointed way provides humankind God's forgiveness of sin is a core Christian tenet. But it does not take away the idea that Jesus came to show us how to live. While it is right to recognize that the full realization of the Kingdom of God will come after this life as the heavenly reality, its partial manifestation here and now must not be ignored.

For many in our time, Christian living becomes a matter of leading a moral and upright life with an emphasis upon personal virtues. Some of us do what we can to promote peace and justice, but are easily deflected by surrounding attitudes of injustice strongly ingrained and discouraged by the overwhelming power struggles of our time. However, when we turn to the Gospel stories and the real, historical Jesus which they show us, we find that it is in regard to issues of peace and justice that Jesus most strongly embodies another way, the way of God in His Kingdom which is near, for the "here and now."

We ought, therefore, to hear what Jesus taught and observe what Jesus did during the three or so years he walked the paths of Palestine. Let us grasp anew what he instructed his disciples to do.

WRY BREAD.....Food for thought with a wry twist
–December 2005

THE PROFITS OF ADVENT

In the season of Advent it is customary to read the Old Testament prophets who lead us to Christmas through the their message of the much anticipated coming of Christ. Advent is the season of prophets. We depend upon the prophets to help us celebrate THE GIFT at Christmas. Advent is also the season of profits–retail profits. Those who sell potential Christmas gifts depend upon the season of Advent and its profits for their own happy celebration of Christmas.

According to news reports Wal Mart, the world's largest retailer, has gotten the prophets and profits of Advent mixed up this year. Apparently to maximize profits during Advent this year Wal Mart made the decision to remove references to the prophecy of Christ's coming in deference to the diversity of religious traditions now present in the American culture. *Happy Holidays*, after all gives everyone good reason to shop during November and December, whereas *Merry Christmas* might limit profit taking from only the Christian segment of the buying public.

However dropping the message of the prophets raised the ire of certain church groups, so much so that they threatened a boycott of Wal Mart. Clearly some of the followers of the prophets were about to reduce profits substantially. Wal Mart got the message and has put *Merry Christmas* back in its stores. Now, apparently the prophets will bring profits.

--Happy Holidays!

–February 2006

HOORAY FOR OUR SIDE?

A few days after the bombing of the Shiite holy shrine

Those who are convinced that God is on their side are politically dangerous, spiritually sterile, intellectually closed, abysmally self absorbed, sinfully arrogant, and frightful bores. Bores because they approach others using a self righteous monologue. Any semblance of honest dialogue is precluded. What is there to discuss if one speaks for God? What more is there to know if one already has the truth. How much more prideful and arrogant and self absorbed could one be than when one claims to speak for God? When one has God down on his or her level, there is no divine resource beyond one's self to approach. This rules out any spiritual quest. One has only to consider the bombing of a Shiite shrine in Iraq and the retaliatory bombing of Sunni mosques to see how politically dangerous religious extremism can be. Having captured God for ones own side is, by definition, religious extremism.

But on the other hand, to try to be on God's side is entirely different. It is, in fact, quite the opposite of having God on our side. Those who seek to align themselves with God, cultivate spirituality as they attempt to discern God's way. They enter into meaningful dialogue with others and are quite willing to learn new truth and to negotiate. Within religious bodies like the church, varying opinions on belief and practice can be discussed and compromise agreements can be reached when those of differing positions recognize that no group, including their own, has God exclusively on its side, but that all contestants are searching for God's way. And what's more, such folk are much more interesting and pleasant to be around.

–February 2006

WHY, OH, WHY. . . . ?

On the evening of February 26th, 2006 some of the world's most accomplished young men and women of many nations from every continent of the globe walked together into the Olympic Stadium in Torino, Italy for the closing ceremony of the 20th Winter Games. Joy was on their faces and comradery united these folk of many religious traditions. This glad event came after days of keen and tense competition when they were pitted against one another as individuals and as nations.

Not many miles south east of Torino tense and deadly violent competition was bringing about its intended inhumane result–the death and maiming of soldiers and civilians of differing beliefs and national heritages, some sent into the pitched battle by their political leaders, others by the clerics of their particular sects. Some of the newly dead had hoped on the day before to return to their homes and families. Others had insanely committed suicide so that others would die by lethal intent.

Images of exultant life in the Olympics have played upon our television screens these past few weeks, while images of dismal and useless death have been thrust into our living rooms as well. The contrast is striking, to say the least.

Why, oh why, don't those who wield the power of nations and exert the persuasion of religion choose life instead of death?

A long time ago on the now bloodied ground of the Middle East, God issued this challenge:

> *See, I have set before you today life and prosperity, death and adversity. If you obey the commandments of the Lord your God. . . by loving the Lord your God, walking in his ways. . .then you shall live. . . Choose life so that you and your descendants may live. . . . (Deuteronomy* 30:15,16,19)

–March 2006

LET THERE BE PEACE
After the annual meeting of Yellowstone Presbytery. . . .

There are two ways to attempt to bring about peace and unity. Those who believe that God is on their side believe, therefore conclude, that unity and peace will come when the others join them, for their's is the way of God. No discussion is needed. As the obedient child must accede to the will of the dominant parent, so those who do not have God on their side must join those who do. This is the way of forced unity and false peace. Jeremiah identified this condition when he spoke these words

> *They have treated the wounds of my people carelessly,*
> *saying, "Peace, peace," when there is no peace. (Jeremiah 6:14)*

A second way to attempt to achieve peace is taken up by those who are seeking to align themselves with God's will–those who are trying to be on God's Side. When we truly seek the will of God, we become aware that God's Way is always to some extent beyond us because of our finite sinfulness. In humility we admit that our understanding is partial and subject to further study. And so we recognize that others, even adversaries, may have some truth and insight from which we can grow in our understanding. This can lead to creative discussion and honest negotiation with others with whom we have had disagreement, *if* the others with whom we seek unity and peace are also *seeking* God's Will.

> "Let there be peace on earth,
> And let it begin with me."

–March 2006

STOP YOUR EARS–SHUT YOUR EYES–AND CLOSE YOUR MIND

—A formula for re-entering the Dark Ages!

A friend of mine recently wrote a letter to the editor of our local newspaper in which he stated, among other things: "Many good Christians have never been able to read and understand the Bible literally." This is a modest claim which a decade ago would have brought little response. Not so today, as evidenced by a letter of rebuttal appearing in the same newspaper a few weeks later. The writer found my friend's statement scary-- to think of him "telling everyone that the Bible, our only physical source of the truth of what we say, cannot be taken literally." The letter of rebuttal makes the assertion that my friend's forsaking of literalism "does not echo the sentiments of many, if any, 'good Christians' that I know."

This exchange in the local paper stands against a backdrop of heated controversy over the issue of what has come to be called "Evolution vs. Intelligent design." It is difficult to fathom such widespread and virile clinging to Medieval thought a half a millennium later. Changes and developments in thought and knowledge in the sixteenth century were resented by the Medieval mind. The newly developing science of geology had the most difficult time emerging according to William Manchester; in *A World Lit Only by Fire,* who wrote "Because of its divine authorship, the biblical account of creation was above criticism."

With its ears stopped, its eyes shut, and its mind closed the Church in the 1500'a sought to keep its faithful in the dark ages, a state of mind so obtuse that "During the Dark Ages literal interpretation of the Bible had led the Church to endorse the absurd treatise that held that the world was a flat, rectangular plane, surmounted by the sky, above which was heaven. Jerusalem was a the center of the rectangle, and nearby was the Garden of Eden, irrigated by the rivers of paradise. (Manchester)

This condition of having ears which do not hear, eyes which fail to see and minds which are locked down, unbelievably, persists among all too many today, five hundred years later. It is bad enough that clinging to biblical literalism keeps one from the truths of science, but sadly this lock down keeps one from perceiving the voice of the Holy Spirit. For when one decides that all God's truth is to be found only in the very words one finds in the Bible, then one is not able hear and see what the Holy Spirit would have us receive as the living Word of God in our own time and place. In so doing one re-enters the Dark Ages.

–June 2006

FREEDOM ISN'T FREE

The day after Memorial Day I passed the Army Recruiting station in the Mall while on my morning walk. A poster in the window proclaimed that *FREEDOM ISN'T FREE.* Nothing was said in so many words about what the nature of the cost is. Only a picture of an army helmet atop a vertically standing rifle. However, everyone knows what the implication is, especially after observing many Memorial Day patriotic celebrations. The cost of freedom, it is assumed, is military conflict and sacrifice. Is warfare the only foundation on which our democracy depends? I think not. Without public education and widespread moral teaching the freedom which we enjoy in our democratic way of life will be eroded by ignorance and moral vacuum. Military sacrifice can keep outside destructive forces at bay, but not internal decay. A significant cost of freedom, I believe, is the tireless devotion and sacrifice of those who teach and those who instill moral values. The commitment of teachers and moral mentors to the common good is a foundation of our democracy every bit as important as the price paid by the military.

WRY BREAD.....Food for thought with a wry twist.
–1985

LIFE IS A BICYCLE

Driving down a familiar street, recently, a passenger in my car remarked, "I didn't know there was a hill in this block." Well, I did, because I had ridden by bike over it many times. When you ride a bike you know where all the hills are. Or do the hills appear only when you are on a bike? Maybe so. There is something strange here, I think. Such a hunch seemed to be supported in my mind last summer while driving through Yellowstone Park. We met a great many oncoming bicyclists and we overtook as many. It seemed that almost all of these were laboriously peddling uphill. Why was that? Surely some must have found some downhill stretches, but we never seemed to see these. Almost everyone–out of breath–struggling mightily–uphill. And some of those hills in Yellowstone aren't mere knolls. I can barely remember any who were on the level, much less on a a downhill ride.

It got me to thinking. Isn't this a sort of picture of life? It seems that everything is and uphill struggle. Like the line from the musical: "Tote that barge, lift that bale!" One problem after another, it seems. Solve one question and another arises. Gotta keep at it, or you'll lose ground and slip back. It would appear that life is a bicycle–peddling uphill

But I still wonder why they were always peddling uphill in the Park. Come to think of it, it must be inherited from the past. It's in the genes of the bicycle. Remember the early models? The diameter of the front wheel was always much bigger than the rear. So the rider always had to peddle uphill. So with us. We started in a primeval cave in an untamed earth. And the cave was probably on the side of a steep hill at that!

Life is a bicycle

–2006

"FAITH IN FICTION"

Do you like to read novels, but you don't appreciate some of the scenes or many of the characters? Did you ever think about the fact that so few characters in modern fiction seem to have much of a faith–Christian Fath, that is? So often the people you meet in today's novels seem to live by secular values and their life style is anything by Christian. Where are the Christians? You can go to a "Christian bookstore" and find novels which literally reek with what I call *artificially forced faith!* When you read these novels you get the feeling that their chief purpose is to bring the reader to an experience of Jesus in a certain way of which the author approves. I have found that many of these novels depict a narrow interpretation of Christian faith and living, which is "foreign to me."

So one wonders where one can go to find stories of Christians people who believe church is important, who try to live by traditional Christian standards of moral behavior, characters who look at the world from a Christian perspective. And perhaps most important stories of people whose faith struggles with the same questions I do! And how do you find stories like that which are enjoyable and entertaining to read as well? Who are some contemporary authors to give us entertaining stories from a Christian point of view. I have found a few such authors whose novels are currently available. Richard Paul Evans who became well-known after publishing The Christmas Box has given us a number of novels such as The Looking Glass, The Last Promise, The Locket and others. Andrew Greeley, a Roman Catholic priest, is a prolific writer, oftentimes featuring Roman Catholic clergy and lay people of Irish descent who live in Chicago or its environs. You'll need tolerance, if not appreciation, for modern Catholocism to enjoy his work. Alexander McCall Smith's No. 1 Ladies Detective Agency series, while not specifically Christian, certainly presents people in Botswana with a God-fearing high moral life style. There are others, I'm sure, but they are far and few between in a midst of murder mysteries, romances, and thrillers of various kinds.

After I completed my first novel, A Place Called Fairhavens, I asked myself what it was I was trying to do. Admittedly my motivation had been to tell a good story which would bring pleasure to the reader. But beyond that, as I thought about "Fairhavens," I realized that in it were people whose faith commitment was Christian and consequently whose behavior and world view revealed the sort of Christian values I hold. People with whom I would enjoy an evening of fellowship and conversation. Then as the next three novels came forth I found in them also characters whose world view and life style were Christian.

–2006

OF MONKEY'S, DINOSAURS, AND BIBLE SCHOLARS

It is eighty-one years and counting since the Bible and science debate was decided in the "Scopes Monkey Trial" in Dayton, Tennessee. Science would be taught in schools and Sunday Schools were free to teach the Bible. Settled? Apparently not. There is mounting pressure from "Bible-believing Christians" around the country to make the Bible science and to relegate *evolution* to the status of unsupportable theory. That is to have Creationism, euphemistically labeled *Intelligent Design*, taught in public school science classes and to have *evolution* taught as a mere theory, replete with numerous limitations. This comes at a time when millions upon millions have been reading the fourteen fear producing novels of the "Left Behind" series by Tim LeHaye and Jerry Jenkins–fiction claiming to follow the Biblical prediction of the end of the world when Jesus will return to earth to lift his followers–Bible-Believing Christians–to heaven and to send those who don't believe to suffer all the ravages of hell during the battle of Armageddon which will take plac in these terrifying "end times."

There seems to be evidence from various polls that almost half of Americans believe in Armageddon as well as a Biblically literal explanation of the creation of the universe in six twenty-four hour days. Many, therefore, deny that there ever were such creatures as dinosaurs, and that monkey's played no part in our development. So far as Biblical scholarship is concerned– who needs it. All you need is the Bible.

On the extreme opposite end of the spectrum a sizeable number of intellectuals have written off the Christian Faith and its Bible as Medieval nonsense. A friend of mine recently attended an adult education class on the subject of science and religion taught by a university faculty member. In the course of the discussion, the teacher, in effect threw up his hands, and said, "Aren't there any Christians who think scientifically?" My friend answered what had been posed as a rhetorical question. "There are, and they are in the 'main line' Churches."

What does say this say about the main line churches? On first consideration this indicates that Christians who accept the conclusions of good science in any field, while understanding and accepting the Bible as a source of truth about God, have been all too quiet about their position. On a deeper level I believe that the widespread proliferation of Biblical literalism and all that goes with it is a result of a failure in Christian Education over the past century.

By and large the main line churches have clergy who have been educated in the field of Biblical interpretation which allows them to pursue and accept the scientific endeavor and to grow in a deepening understanding of the Bible as the Word of God to humankind clothed in the words and thought patterns of its writers ranging from 900 BCE to around 100 AD, long before the advent of scientific discovery and rational enlightenment. But this level of scientific and Biblical understanding, apparently has not been adequately taught. The result has been that many main line members have gone over to churches and preachers who hold to a literal interpretation of the Bible, while at the same time others with a more sophisticated intellectual preference have simply left the churches, concluding that all Christians are narrowly literalistic and woefully behind the times.

When those of us in the main line churches wonder why we have lost so many members in the last few decades, perhaps we should look to our failure to educate people in a Biblical understanding fit for the twenty-first century.

–2006

WHERE IS GOD?

The issue of Religion and Politics is big these days. One's opinion on this issue depends upon where God is in one's thinking. Against the traditional American backdrop of the separation of church and state, what appears to be the ever-tightening alliance of the "religious right" with the present Republican administration is seen by many who are not on the religious or political right as dangerous. The danger is that extreme religious positions may influence, or worse yet, determine U.S. policy unwisely and to our own detriment. Many on the religious right believe the scenario presented in the fictional "Left Behind" series, which predicts the return of Christ to take his own to heaven, while bringing everlasting condemnation to those others who have not accepted Christ. According to this imagined interpretation of the end of times, Christ's return will come only after great tribulation including the battle of Armageddon after which the Jews will be returned to their homeland of Israel. This view point, when applied to the conflicts the Middle East, has very dire implications. The crushing of all who oppose Israel is believed to be God's will, and the Iraq war is seen as a step in that divine direction. To say the least we ought not to allow some overly embellished fiction based upon a certain interpretation of a few verses in the Bible taken literally determine U.S. foreign policy. This is but one example of placing **God on one's side.**

Abraham Lincoln resisted those who tried to persuade him that God occupied a certain side or policy decision. In 1862 he wrote: 'The will of God prevails. In great contests each party claims to act in accordance with the will of God. Both *may* be, and one *must* be wrong. God cannot be *for*, and *against* the same thing at the same time. In the present civil war it is quite possible that God's purpose is something different from the purpose of either party."

Lincoln understood God's position to be beyond particular party politics or specific domestic or foreign policies with a will and intention which we are to seek, rather than to commandeer. This view-point places **God beyond human life.**

Many of those who decry any involvement of religion in public affairs deny the relevance of religion to anything but to individual people's lives. This view-point relegates any particular god or religious system to personal opinion. Whatever god one wants to follow resides in one's own self and consciousness. **God is one's mind**, and should have nothing to do with public affairs. Other people and nations may have other god's in their minds or traditions, or they may have no god.

There seems to be yet another position for God in American life. That is **God as ceremonial.** In the rituals and celebrations of public life God is often summoned to bless what we are building or doing. God is mentioned on our currency, the Senate chaplain prays over that body once in a while, and we sometimes mention God at the end of official speeches. In a deeper sense we seek God's help in desperate situations and thank God in moments of exultation.

How one relates religion to politics depends upon where God is!

–2006

TOO LITTLE–TOO LATE

As a result of an alleged massacre of Iraqi civilians by U.S. Marines the government has decided to institute a new training program for miliary personnel. The new training is to teach the troops "core values" of what is moral, legal and ethical. This is designed to address the supposed shortcomings on the part of our troops in the event the allegations are proved true. Presumably this new training will keep us from doing such horrific things again. Sadly for the innocent Iraqis this is too little and too late. Perhaps also for others in Iraq and elsewhere who have not as yet been similarly treated.

After-the-fact pondering leads one to ask *where were the morals and ethics* in our society before the alleged massacre? Furthermore, could it be that our passion for separating church and state with its side-effect of unwillingness to teach values in public education has left a fatal void which we are now trying to fill with too little too late?

WRY BREAD...... Food for thought with a wry twist.
–June 5, 2006

ABSOLUTELY YOUR LAST CHANCE

As I write this there remains about a half a day left to win $10 million on an investment of a mere $100, and you can do it on line. BetUS.com It's as easy at that. Think what you could do if you had ten million. And the odds aren't too bad as such things go–100,000 to 1. And if gambling bothers you, rest assured this is in the Bible. It's right there in Revelation 13:18–the magic number 666. That means that if you bet on the side of the Bible you'll be assured of ten million. Think what a future you'll have with that much money.

Now here's the plan. Everyone knows that 666 is the sign of the Beast, and the Beast means the end of the world and so you don't even have to be good at math to know that June 6, 2006 is 06-06-06, and 666 is the Beast and the Beast's coming is the END of time. You can bet on it, then, that the END will come on June 6, 2006. Hurry online and place your bet of $100 that the world will end tomorrow, June 6, 2006, and it's a sure thing–by the end of tomorrow you'll be rich. But this is absolutely your last chance! Or not quite, but then again June 6, 3006 is a long time to wait for another sure chance.

Better to get yours tomorrow when the proper authorities are assured that the world really did end and you would have been entitled to $10,000,000, but then wouldn't it just be your luck that all the banks would be closed 06-06-06–permanently, but then-also-- you can't take it with you, anyhow.

Might there be some serious lessons here? Yes, I think there is.

- Reading the Bible literally gets you on the wrong track.
- Getting rich, though appealing, is ultimately futile.
- Gambling is dumb.

–September 11, 2006

FOR THESE, WHO WILL TOLL THE BELL?
—a lament

Today across my country bells have been tolling, one ring after the reciting of each name from the list of almost three thousand who lost their lives on "9/11" five years ago. When a name is read and the sound of the bell is heard, a father or a mother, a son or a daughter, a wife, a husband, or a brother or a sister remembers and relives that shattering moment of grief when violence from afar was brought upon us within our shores. For each of these whom we have lost, someone has tolled a bell of remembrance–a small but poignant act of devotion to the innocent ones who died. All these were our children. We know their names. And they were children of God.

But sadly there are others for whom no bell is tolled. More than our three thousand, all children of God whose names we do not know. For these, who will toll the bell? These also died since the dawn of September 11, 2001. They were the innocent ones killed in Iraq. Someone's son and his entire family who were wiped out when their house was bombed. The small child out in the street playing at the wrong time in the wrong place, who will never return home for supper again. The father who was killed when his shop was destroyed by a misguided bomb. The mother who was hanging out clothes to dry and will never return to her home. The brother applying for training for the security force in Iraq, killed with the others waiting to be inducted. The young couple just married when a suicide bomber crashed their wedding reception. And there are others still. Each with loved ones who remember and relive their shattering moments of grief when violence from afar took away their sons and daughters, mothers and fathers, wives and husbands, brothers and sisters. For these who will toll the bell?

> *Forgive me, Lord, I do not even know their names, so how can I toll the bell. But You know each name, for each one of these is your child, Lord. And for each lost child you grieve. And I do not even know their names. So how can I toll the bell of grief and remembrance? Forgive me, Lord.*

For these, who will toll the bell?

WHAT'S IN THE NAME "COMMUNITY" CHURCH?

The two churches which I served in Wyoming the 1950's were only ten miles apart, which for Wyoming is unusual when and ten miles is closer than next door. But they were miles apart in other ways. Their names were also very close but so different in a quite significant way. One was the Presbyterian Community Church of Yoder, while the other was the Community Presbyterian Church of Hawk Springs. Guess which one is no longer affiliated with the Presbyterian Church? the one which chose to place "Community" in front of "Presbyterian."

Now fifty years later the prevailing trend favors the Hawk Springs forsaking of its denominational connection. I find it a troubling trend that many Presbyterian congregations are relegating the name "Presbyterian" to their legal papers and erasing it from their signs and letterheads. Their rationale seems to be that many people today do not retain any denominational identity, let alone loyalty, and that they will be attracted to churches which have relinquished such names and proclaim themselves "Community" churches.

That may well be, but I tend to doubt it. What really bothers me is that with this relegation of the name "Presbyterian" to the scrap heap of history, so also the regard for Presbyterian connection is also spurned. With a *less government is the best government* attitude I believe there is trend here toward rejecting the authority of the Presbyterian system. A creeping congregationalism dashing head-long away from any denominational claims, I fear.

–October 3,2006

TWO WORLDS COLLIDING

This morning in Pennsylvania a group of men and women from an Amish community in the town of Nickel Mines waits prayerfully at the hospital bedside of a thirteen year old girl of their community. She is one of the innocent victims of an enraged and violent man who entered her Amish school yesterday carrying three firearms which he used to kill four of her classmates before violently killing himself. A heart-breaking tragedy under any circumstances but one which is even more poignant for occurring in this community of the Amish Christians, so totally committed to non-violence of any kind.

In this most sad of events we see two worlds colliding. Their world and – I am ashamed to say -- our world. Ours is a world in which the manufacture, distribution, and use of firearms is huge and horrendous, both for bloody warfare and for personal killing. The world of the Amish is one in which there are no guns, except for necessary hunting, a world in which violence is completely avoided.

Nation-wide attention is focused upon Lancaster County, Pennsylvania with intrusive television shots of horse-drawn wagons, and "simple folk" in their straw hats and hand made long dresses assembled outside their school, so recently the scene of death by gun-shot. Some media commentators have been quick to point out the irony of this collision of the simple, old fashioned and peaceful world of the Amish largely unknown to the viewer with the *real* world–our world, that is. The real world in which two other school deadly shootings in less than a week. One wonders if some haven't thought, if not said. "Wake up, get with it. This is what life is really made of! Your idealism won't get you very far in our real world."

And yet many of us in our violent world claim to follow the Prince of Peace. Do we *really?*

In which of these two worlds colliding is Jesus really Prince? This tragic collision begs each of us to assess his or her own personal answer to the question of violence.

The community of Amish in Nickel Mines follows the Mennonite tradition which for centuries as confessed its practice of non-violence in terms something like this:

> *"As followers of Jesus, we participate in his ministry of peace and justice. He has called us to find our blessing in making peace and seeking justice. We do so in the spirit of gentleness, willing to be persecuted for righteousness' sake. As disciples of Christ. . . the same Spirit that empowered him.*
>
> *Jesus also empowers us to love enemies, to forgive rather that to seek revenge, to practice right relationships, to rely on the community of faith to settle disputes, and to resist evil without violence.* (Confession of Faith in a Mennonite Perspective, pp 81-82, Herald Press, Scottdale, Pa, 1995)

Two worlds colliding: one is small, considered to be out of date and out of touch; the other is huge, all pervasive, contemporary. Which world shall be ours?

–October 9, 2006

A CHRISTENING? . . . I THINK NOT!

In yesterday's Bozeman Daily Chronicle, Sunday morning readers were greeted with a headline which reads: ***Bushes attend christening of aircraft carrier.*** From what sources this headline originated, I do not know. But according to my understanding of Christ, the Prince of Peace, by whom any true Christening is to take place, whoever considered the ceremonial naming of a new nuclear powered aircraft carrier a CHRISTENING unwittingly committed a tragic blasphemy. This warship can carry over eighty combat aircraft, each of which is an efficient agent of death and destruction. Certainly not my idea of anything the Prince of Peace is apt be launching.

The Bush family attended a naming ceremony last week by which this massive gray hulk was named. THE USS GEORGE H. W. BUSH. By any stretch of my imagination this was not a Christening. Perhaps the only saving grace in this article was the fact that the Chronicle did not capitalize the word "christening."

On this solemn occasion President Bush described the capacity of this carrier to wage war thus: "She is unrelenting, she is unshakable she is unyielding, she is unstoppable." One can wonder, if perhaps those four strong adjectives were conscious or unconscious self-descriptions. He then went on to imply that he had just described Barbara Bush. Like mother like son?

–November 14, 2006

WHEN WILL IT EVER END?

National Public Radio, this morning, had a segment which covered a training program for soldiers preparing to go to Iraq. The latest terrorist weapons and tactics were demonstrated so that our troops would have some warning of potential violence against them. In the course of this training one of the trainers commented upon the seemingly endless threat we face. "It will never end, " he said, "until he just doesn't want to kill you."

I think what the leader of this training program said more or less off the cuff, is, in fact, *the answer,* much more profound than he realized. To repeat the phrase used on last night's national news, the MESS in Iraq will end only when we don't want to kill anymore. And that goes for the MESS everywhere else in the world – from the deadly land mines hidden in the Columbian farmer's field to the wrenching famine in the Sudan, and horrible genocide wherever one finds it today.

The answer is so simple, and yet, given how we view the world, so impossible. If we could just get to the point where we don't want to kill anymore! But, the awful reality is that we do want to kill. In fact we think that the way to stop the killing is to kill. What a subverted thought pattern that is. We think the way to stop the enemy is to kill him, the way to stop crime is to send the criminal to the electric chair, the way to construct a perfect society is to remove violently those who are different. Walter Wink names this "The Myth of Redemptive Violence."

He elaborates. "It enshrines the belief that violence saves, that war brings peace, that might makes right. It is one of the oldest continuously repeated stories in the world . . (It) is the real myth of the modern world." (Walter Wink, The Powers That Be, p.42, Galilee Book-Doubleday-1998)

Not to want to kill anymore goes against the very powerful operating principal of our time. To act upon that desire places one at odds with his or her nation and society. Such an unpopular notion just might even "put you on a Cross!" It did for Jesus.

But there it is! When will it ever end? When I just don't want to kill anymore.

WRY BREAD.....Food for thought with a wry twist
–December 1989

"BY THEIR FRUITS YE SHALL KNOW THEM"

Did you know that one of the traditional Christmas symbols is the apple? And did you know that the apple is a traditional symbol of human sin? Remember the Garden of Eden? *God hath said, ye shall not eat of it, neither shall ye touch it, lest ye die.* (Genesis 3:3 AV) It has long assumed that the forbidden fruit which our first parent ate was the apple. So, when you hang an ornament shaped like an apple on your Christmas tree you are reminding yourself of the sin from which the Christ Child came to earth to save us,

I don't know about you, but I did not know all this until this year's batch of Christmas commercials were aired on the radio, paid for by various local businesses. You know, how you get nice Christmas messages in between holiday songs which often conclude with something like, ". . . . from your friends at Ajax Welding Supply for a very Merry Christmas to you and your family ." I always thought these messages were assigned at random to advertisers, who had no hand in what the message would say on their behalf. However now I wonder, since one commercial explaining the apple as a Christmas symbol was signed off: "Courtesy of *so and so's* Bingo Parlor and Casino, wishing you a most blessed Christmas." How appropriate for the owners and operators of your friendly neighborhood gambling establishment, to tell you about the apple, which you will remember is a symbol for sin! Further fulfillment of the snake's advice in Genesis story, that it would be OK to eat the apple and that they wouldn't die like it said. Thus an implied; approval of gambling at *so and so's* casino, or any other,

When I was a little kid my friend, Ricky, whose dad was a policeman, had a confiscated "one armed bandit" and had put it in his recreation room. I remember that there were apples pictured on its rolling dials. Now I know why, thanks to *so and so's* carefully chosen commercial which explained about the apple

However, did you notice that the Bible didn't say it was an apple? Might have been a pomegranate. But, then, who would know what a pomegranate looks like hanging on a tree?.

–January 11, 2007

"THE PLACE WHERE I WORSHIP . . . ."

Our town has joined many other communities across the country in arguing over whether to put up the Ten Commandments in a public setting. While in the midst of this controversy, it is helpful to read the Ten Commandments and then ask, "Do we really mean to put all that up somewhere for all to see?" I suspect that most people think of lying, stealing and adultery when they think "Ten Commandments." There are seven other commandments, some of which we may not want to post!

Consider numbers 1 and 2:

> *You shall have no other gods before me. You shall not make for yourself an idol, whether in the form of anything that is in heaven above or that is on the earth beneath, or that is in the water under the earth. (Including snow?) You shall not bow down to them or worship them*

Most, I think, will agree that this refers to anything which we devise which takes the place of God and becomes the object of our worship. Well, there are a lot of such alternatives from which to choose from these days. Many pet projects and favorite activities qualify as idols. And we do not really want to publicly display any divine directives which would spoil our particular enjoyments.

Some years ago a popular song declared, "*The place where I worship was built by the hand of God.*" This, of course, referred to the great outdoors–nature–where during numerous outdoor recreational activities one would worship God, instead of going to church to do so. While nature itself is "built by the hand of God," ones golf game isn't. No, it was created by some ancient Scot, whose name is no longer known. But his disciples are legion. And perhaps fly-fishing originated with another unknown Scotsman. I'm not sure who erected skiing as a pleasurable idol. But it qualifies.

An article in today's local newspaper reports on an increasingly popular Sunday activity–cross country skiing. One of the owners of a local facility which provides for practicing and teaching this particular Sunday option is quoted in the article, in which she extolls this activity in the following words: *"It's a great family activity because it reaches across all generations. It's something you can do all your life."*

No one in this town would want to carve in a stone erected in a public place the following: "*You shall not cross-country ski.*" So we had better think twice about putting up those Ten Commandments, at least not the first two.

And, by the way, *"It's a great family activity because it reaches across all generations. It's something you can do all your life,"* describes church life and worship quite nicely!

–January 2007

THE GREAT DIVIDE

In its December 18, 2006 "U.S. News and World Report" offered a Christmas issue of sorts with a familiar Madonna and child on its cover and announcing its lead article as *"In Search of the Real Jesus–New research questions whether he was more teacher than savior."* Jay Tolson, the writer of the cover article, reports on the current scholarship being done on the newly re-discovered suppressed writings of second century Christian Gnostics, which were branded "heretical" by the hierarchy of the Church at the time. Tolson comments on the controversy which this reintroducing to Gnosticism has sparked: "Today there are many scholars, theologians and popular writers who promote the Gnostic perspective as a liberating antidote to close-minded dogmatism, but there are also many others who denounce it as a pernicious and destructive influence."

In 1979 Elaine Pagels published The Gnostic Gospel as a result of her scholarship, which became immensely popular. Tolson explains the popularity of her work: "In an America still reeling from Watergate, still distrustful of authority and institutions, and still shaken by the liberating intensities of the 1960's, here was a book that argued that early Christianity contained a multitude of diverse interpretations and movements–or at least did so until the leaders of the orthodox church succeeded in suppressing them as heresies."

Pointing to the ready reception of this ancient view-point Tolson observes: "Name many of the issues that fuel our cultural politics today–authority vs. individual freedom, fixed moral precepts vs. moral relativism, religion vs. spirituality–and you can find usable precedents in that long-distant conflict between Gnostic Christians and their orthodox foes."

For many, both scholars and general readers alike, the re-discovery of Gnostic ideas challenges traditional Christian belief in the divinity of Jesus and conviction that it is through Christ that we are given salvation. The uncovering of additional documents and other gospels from the early days of Christianity has put into question the authority of the Bible when the development of the canon is seen as full of politically based decisions. Thus the right of the early church bishops to give us some of the available books while banning others, challenges the authority of the Church to determine Christian doctrine. The net effect of these challenges is to reduce Christian beliefs to human formed ideas and opinions.

We are experiencing in these discussions. what might be called the Great Divide. The opposing words in Tolson's article which best set the boundaries for the divide are: *authority vs. individual freedom.* Is one's source of truth outside ones own self, or does one find in ones own self the means to find ultimate truth by which to understand the world and how to live. In other words where is your god (authority)– outside yourself or within.

On one side of the great divide one is lifted and carried along by a power greater than onesself. On the other side one does one's own lifting and guiding. This view-point might be called *a bootstrap theology,* while the other is a *theology of dependence.* On one side Christians look to God as revealed through scripture and tradition (Bible and Church) for life and truth. Those on the other side conclude in effect: *We looked for God and found divinity within ouselves.*

–January 2007

"GOLD IS WHERE YOU FIND IT"

Two mythical sentences have been used to describe conversations early day gold miners exchanged in many a make-shift mining town in territorial Montana. *"Thar's gold in them thar hills."*. . . "*Gold is where you find it.*" And *"Somewhere when you least expect it!"* one might add.

In a way reading serious popular fiction can be like that. When reading a novel merely for pleasure one sometimes stumbles on a gold nugget– an episode in which redemption happens. And a story told for the fun of it becomes a mini-gospel. Sometimes between the alluring paper-back covers we find the good news of the power of love to transform lives.

Nicholas Sparks' novel, A Walk to Remember is one of *them thar hills* in which gold is to be found. Set in 1959 it is the story of a rich high school boy, Landon Carter, who runs with the wild crowd in his school, with those who delight in ridiculing the straight laced Baptist preacher and his Bible-carrying daughter, Jamie Sullivan. While Landon had known Jamie from their childhood she had always been perceived as"different" because of her closeness to her father and his pius and morally narrow ways. A series of circumstances, beyond Landon's control, he and Jamie thrown together in such a way as to cause Landon to see her as she really is. The nugget of gold in this story is that ultimately Jamie's child-like goodness touches Landon and their resulting relationship transforms his life. In traditional religious terms Jamie becomes an instrument of Landon's redemption. And his redemption brings about his reconciliation with others in his life.

This vein of gold can be discovered in other novels of Nicholas Sparks. One can find a similar theme in his recent novel, Dear John, when the careless and sometimes violent life of the main character is given new purpose and sensitivity to others through a life-changing relationship with, a young woman with a passion for helping others.

There is this kind of gold to be found in John Grisham's The Testament. When a prestigious law firm sends an alcoholic partner to find the recipient of a huge estate, who turns out to be a courageous missionary in the jungles of South America, he not only finds her but she helps him to find himself. Once again the nugget of gold is the redemption of a person through an authentic relationship of love with another person.

If a novel depicts human life authentically it will tell the reader of redemption, for there are many examples of redemptive activity in the lives around us. You just have to look and know what you are looking for.

Gold is where you find it. Serious popular fiction is one gulch in which you'll discover rich deposits of gold. *God is where you find him.*

–January 2007

THE NOVELIST AS EVANGELIST

In the past few weeks I have been re-reading three of the novels of the popular Nicholas Sparks. The impact of these three stories upon my spirit has been quite considerable and very positive. After reading *Message in a Bottle* I found myself having a new appreciation of significant relationships with people in my life and feeling impelled to relate to each one more lovingly. In this story Sparks brings Theresa Osborne and Garret Blake into a deep and loving relationship. Each, having been emotionally hurt, finds in the other, healing and hope. So real are the lives of these two, and so authentic is the relationship which grows between them that the reader is led to participate in a depth of love which can spread to the reader's own relationships as well. Or, at least such was my experience.

And then when I came to the end of the story in *Nights in Rodanthe* I experienced the same response. In this story, Adrienne and Paul Flanner, through their deep love, bring life transformation to each other. Because of their love for each other, each is able to relate to others more authentically.

In *A Walk to Remember* the unlikely relationship of Landon Carter with Jamie Sullivan brings a new and transformed life to each of them. As is also the case with both Theresa and Garret and Adrienne and Paul the untimely loss through death makes the deep impact of their love even more influential in the life of the reader, I think being privileged to feel the love depicted in each of these stories, and to realize that my relationships have become the better for it, I suggest that Nicholas Sparks has functioned in my life as an evangelist.

To apply the term, evangelist to a novelist is to invite destructive misunderstanding. I have discovered that many so called Christian novels are blatantly evangelistic, in that the story involves the intentional conversion of one or more characters to faith in Jesus Christ, characters in the story, who at the outset are sinners without any care for Christ, but who through the evangelistic witnessing of another character are won to Christ.

This is not what I mean by referring to the novelist as evangelist. Rather, I mean that the novelist, in presenting authentic human beings in authentic situations, can show us love which is deep and real, and life changing. In this sense I believe the novelist brings us the *evangel,* the good news of love, which has its source in God.

I believe, furthermore, that God is at work in the writings of some serious novelists, bringing God's love into the lives of their readers. Certainly I attest to the fact that God did that for me as I read some of the novels of Nicholas Sparks. For this I thank God, and God's unwitting instrument–the writer of an authentic human story.

–January 2007

WHO'S PAYING MY RENT?

Sparked by the recent discoveries of other gospels, such as *The Gospel of Thomas*, the authority of the Bible in its present sixty-six book form is being challenged by some students of religion, both professional academics and popular "hangers on." This challenge manifests itself at two points in particular: the canonization process by which the early Church approved the "official" books of the Bible; and the assumed unity of opinion in the Christian church from the beginning.

Once it is alleged that there is probably as much truth in literary material which was rejected as in the Bible, and when it is shown that there always have been differing, if not conflicting, opinions among early Christians, the unique authority of the Bible can be severely compromised.

In evaluating this challenge it seems to me that there is a similarity here to what we have come to believe is a defect in scientific research which is funded by groups wanting certain answers which support their endeavors or products. It is important to ask of such research, "Who's paying the rent for your laboratory space? In other words, "What is your starting point?" Your hidden agenda.

It is my observation that those who have been schooled in a strong Biblical literalism, and are now reacting to such an autocratic doctrine, are apt to swing far to the left, so to speak, collecting evidence which supports the premise that there is little or no particular authority to the words of scripture. So far as containing ultimate truth, the Bible is seen as no different from any other written source. Strong reaction to years of the literalist suppression of thought and inquiry is "paying the rent," so to speak.

If one has invested the words of the Bible with divine authority, and then one discovers that those words are defective in some ways, one is apt to lose hold of any authority, except, perhaps, ones own opinions.

The short-sightedness of both the literalist and the reactor is that both are hung up on the words of the Bible itself. In 1945 a well-respected Biblical scholar and translator was quoted as follows:

> *Christianity began as a religion not of the letter but of the spirit, and inherited a rich religious literature; moreover its keen apocalyptic expectations were unfavorable to literary composition.* (Edgar J. Goodspeed)

This observation is amplified by Karl Barth, the early twentieth century Swiss theologian when he writes "The words of the Bible bear witness to the Word of God." This means to me that God "speaks," or better yet, *acts* in life of the reader of Scripture, no matter how defective in one way or another the particular passage of the Bible may be.

In traditional doctrinal language this is *Inspiration.* H. Richard Niebuhr, An American theologian says it this way:

> *In Protestant doctrine the "testimony of the Holy Spirit". . . must accompany the reading of the word if there is to be true inspiration. . . .*(H. Richard Niebuhr)

Lest the subjective dimension of this process lead us astray, Niebuhr adds:

> *Among the criteria employed by religious thought to distinguish true from false inspiration the most important are: (1) the consistency of the product of the inspiration not only in itself but also and primarily with accepted norms, ie, with the moral laws, the "spirit of Jesus Christ," the Scriptures, the common understanding of the community.*

> *(2) the truth of prediction. (3) disinterestedness, that is the extent to which personal interests and opinions are absent or negated in the "inspired" utterance. (4) intelligibility might be added as a fourth criterion of the validity of inspiration. . . .* (H. Richard Niebuhr)

Well, then, who should pay the rent? What is your starting point? If your starting point is a desire to discount the authority of the Bible because the total truth of every word in it was drilled into you, then you will probably miss the deeper truth of the Bible. But if your starting point is that of the Bible itself: *In the beginning God. . . . (Genesis 1:1),* then you will find God's own revelation. Who is paying my rent? God!

WRY BREAD.....Food for thought with a wry twist
–January 26,2007

LEFT BEHIND BY THE LEFT

Recently I was told of a bumper sticker seen around town which sounds humorous at first, but which has a sad side to it. *Don't pray in my school and I won't think in your church.* While I suppose the purveyors of this cryptic message intend to make a statement opposing prayer in public schools, the far more insidious claim here is that *Christians don't think.* My challenge to such an opinion is often frustrated by noisy evidence supporting the bumper sticker's message that Christians are intellectually behind the times.

This morning's Chronicle carried a Washington Post article on the front page which reports an angry protest to the School Board in Federal Way, Washington. Written by e-mail by a parent opposing the showing of Al Gore's film documenting global warming to his seventh grade daughter's class, the parent, who's first name is given as Frosty, identifies himself as an evangelical Christian. As such, he claims that global warming is "one of the signs" of Judgement Day coming soon with the return of Jesus Christ. I guess the implication is that we ought not to tamper with any divine signs.

Is it any wonder that thinking people with a scientific understanding of the world often have some very negative thoughts about Christians, especially in regard to our ability to think. And along with Al Gore many such intellectuals are to the left of center on many social and environmental issues. The sad result often is that the church has been *left behind by the left.*

Could it be that the loud and often angry shouts from the RIGHT are leaving the LEFT behind?

Or that global warming is too awful a threat to us--especially if you have a name like Frosty?

–January 27,2007

CYNICAL ABOUT THE PINNACLE

One of the more notorious developers in our county has just announced that he will build the most expensive spec house in the world some forty-five miles or so up the Gallatin River in the mountains toward Yellowstone Park. Designed by a local architectural firm to be completed in twelve to fourteen months, he will have it on the market for *one hundred fifty-five million dollars.* ($155,000,000). He has made his project known nationally and has already been contacted by interested cash buyers. This ten bedroom house will have 53,000 square feet of living space–44 times the amount of living space in my house. The developer, who is on *Forbes Magazine's* list of the richest people in our country, plans to call this new house *The Pinnacle,* which I would allege has autobiographical overtones.

Twenty-nine centuries ago Amos was concerned about some of his neighbors who lived on a pinnacle, so to speak. Or rather, God, was concerned! For Amos, after all, spoke the Lord's word to Israel:

> *You have built houses of hewn stone. . .lie on beds of ivory. . . lounge on couches and eat lambs from the flock and calves from the stall. . .but are not grieved over the ruin of your country.* (From Amos 5 and 6)

Ruin? Yes. To name just one relevant contrast: The number of homeless, many of whom are working, is growing at a shameful rate. $155,000,000 is enough provide 15,500 house trailers at $10,000 each.

This wouldn't solve the problem nationwide, but it would surely go along way toward caring for the homeless in the entire state of Montana.–and then some, I should think.

The balance between private gain and the common good is out of whack, and I'm not sure that the $15,000,000 poured onto the ground in the mountains south of here would find its way to the homeless, even if the Pinnacle project were to be abandoned.

Forgive me for being cynical about the Pinnacle.

–January 30, 2007

HE GAVE US A NEW OPERATING SYSTEM

Microsoft put on the market yesterday a new operating system making a great deal of hoopla over its introduction.

If we take seriously what Jesus actually did and how he related to people during the time he was with us historically, we will be introduced to a new operating system for our lives. If we believe that he calls us to follow him as his disciples, then we will begin to see how he wants us to act in society. He calls us to an alternative way of relating to other individuals and groups. The Gospels report that Jesus began his public ministry with the proclamation "The Kingdom of God has come near."(Mark1:15 NRSV) However else the kingdoms of this world act, Jesus comes presenting and embodying a new way, the way of God. His own life reveals the Kingdom of God into which he calls us. Therefore we must find the real Jesus in the real world as told to us in the Gospels. When we turn to the Gospel stories with this expectancy we find a man whose radically new approach to others and to society so threatened and enraged the those who followed the existing way and were embedded in the prevailing power structures, that they killed him. Then when we take seriously Jesus' command to us to "take up our cross and follow him," we become uncomfortable thinking what may well be ahead for us as well!

A new operating system, not just for Geeks, but for you and me too.

THE ONE WAY NOT TO LIVE IS ONE-WAY

One of my pet peeves is to be shown a TV interview of a person who responds to the interviewer's questions while wearing sunglasses, making it impossible for the viewer to observe the eyes of the person interviewed. I think that limits the clarity and the value of the interview.

Sculptors in ancient Greece could transform rigid, cold, lifeless stone into what appeared to be soft, warm lively personages. Thus statues of the gods came to life under the adept chisel of the artist–except for the eyes! These were round, blank, lifeless slugs. The eyes of such statues have remained for centuries–stone cold and opaque–unseeing and unrevealing. I guess only God can make an eye!

In a contrary sort of way modern technology can transform a living eye into what appears to be a cold plastic blob, like an ancient Greek eye of stone–quite unrevealing. One-way reflecting sunglasses! When you wear these, instead of eyes you'll show two dark slugs, and you'll look a bit like Orphan Annie, if not like a Greek god.. With one way sunglasses you can see others--but you'll not be seen by others. "I can see you, but you can't see me–so there!" or worse yet, "I'll see what I want to see, and you won't be able to affect me by so much as a glance!"

It appears to me that one-way reflective sunglasses are a metaphor for one of the problems of our world. Two way communication is so often missing. We are apt to carry on double monologues–each talking without listening. One person with dark blanks for eyes talking at another person with dark blanks for eyes.

From families suffering from inadequate communication to volatile misunderstanding among nations; from international terrorism, to campaign slogans and political double-speak, it might be said that life these days is a ONE-WAY glass. And really the one way NOT to live is one-way.

And, oh yes, statues with stone eyes also have hearts of stone. Something to reflect upon!

–February 2007

TUTORING THE TOURIST

The school shooting in an Amish School in Lancaster County, Pennsylvania brought the fickle focus of the public upon the Amish and the strange ways of this Christian group. Most everyone had been aware of the old fashioned dress of the Amish with the black brimmed hats of the men and the long plain dresses of the women, as well as their use of the horse and buggies instead of the automobile. These strange customs have brought many a tourist to Lancaster County to observe the Amish. But perhaps the strangest behavior of all was broadcast far and wide after the school shootings. And that was the forgiveness which the Amish families extended to the family of the murderer of their children. This "unreasonable" act was difficult for those outside the Amish community to understand, much less to accept. Religious journals and other magazines published articles which sought to explain such acts of forgiveness. Now, not just tourists, but people seeking a deeper understanding of the Amish must be ready to learn from them--- the tourist would be tutored!

And so it was, that when the adult education committee of our church asked the congregation what they wanted to study, some replied, "The Amish." A week or so ago I volunteered to lead such a class, and ever since I have been tutored by the Amish, as I have studied this Christian group with "strange ways." I have found that when you get over being a tourist, focusing upon the buggies and bonnets, and cut to their core values there are four root causes of their life-style which have emerged in my consciousness as deeply Christian, four values those of us

Christian "outsiders" ought to prayerfully consider for ourselves. Values which, if leading to practice would go a long way toward addressing some of the most pressing ills in our society and throughout the world as well.

The core values of the Amish, as I see it, are these four: ***submission, separation, simplicity, and spurning violence.*** Let me explain.

As I try to understand the Amish life-style and ethic, I see *submission* to be the underlying foundation. Submitting to God in as full an obedience to Jesus Christ as possible. Jesus' teaching and example become the blue-print for living. The church then develops an ethic and life-style which it believes best reflects the teachings Jesus. Furthermore, submitting one's individuality to the life and ways of one's church determines a great deal of one's behavior as it conforms to the norms of the group.

Separation from the surrounding culture comes to the Amish community as a result of the fact that the thought and behavior of the culture outside the Amish community do not appear to the Amish to reflect an obedience to the teaching and example of Jesus. Furthermore, some kinds of contact with the surrounding culture with its divergent values is seen as endangering the full submission to Jesus as the church embodies it.

Simplicity follows as a result of giving up one's own tendency toward pride and ostentation to any degree in order to live on an equal level with the others in the group, in submission to the example of simple humility of Jesus. One does no put oneself forward or above others in any way.

Spurning violence is a logical extension of not putting oneself forward or above others. And it is a result of submission to Jesus who taught peace and love instead of the urge to dominate others, and to engage in aggressive thought and behavior. That is to spurn violence in any form.

Taken together it seems to me that the values and ethic of the Amish would go a long way toward addressing many of the overwhelming problems facing us today: conspicuous consumption, sometimes labeled obscene; extreme adulation of celebrities; ruthless competition in business and personal life; interpersonal abuse of one kind or another;

crime of all sorts, especially murder and rape; terrorism and mass bombing of innocents; escalating warfare among nations as well as between religious and ethnic groups; poverty, hunger and starvation, and inexcusable disparity in the distribution of life supporting resources world-wide.

Yes, I think, seriously seeking to follow the teaching and example of Jesus, as the Amish do, will be the start for us in facing these ominous ills of our world today. Instead of tourists merely visiting Lancaster County let us be tutored by the Amish. Instead of merely taking a tour of the country Jesus Christ came to show us, let us be truly tutored by Jesus, so that we may be citizens of a new age of peace and love

–March 2007

"STICKS AND STONES. . . " AND BONES

Well, there's another "flap" brewing regarding the identity of Jesus. Once again coming from the popular press and the entertainment industry. Like Dan Brown's *The DaVinci Code* this new entry into the ongoing discussion is a film called, I think, *The Tomb of Jesus.* Based upon an archeological discovery of an ancient ossuary, which purportedly holds the bones of Jesus and of others in his family, including those of Mary Magdalene.

Some use this as another assault on Jesus' divinity. Another "aha, see there, he was just a man." The juicy reference to Mary Magdalene is used as proof that Jesus was married, much like a similar reference in *The DaVinci Code.* Recently, having seen again a stage performance of *Jesus Christ Superstar,* the phrase from the song which Mary Magdalene sings, "He's just a man," is ringing in my ears as I ponder the current film.

When I first heard about this rendition of part of the Jesus story, my reaction was to interpret this as a denial of the resurrection. After all, if they found his bones, he could not have been raised from the dead! Or could he? The apostle, Paul asserts that Jesus body, and ours, is buried a physical body, and raised a spiritual body. So, his bones could very well have stayed buried and later placed in an ossuary. His resurrection was something apart from old bones.

Thus, I believe, the essence of Jesus Christ remains unharmed by the discovery of his bones—if they are, indeed his. "Sticks and stones will break my bones, but words can never hurt me." So goes the childhood refrain. In other words, the very essence of each of us is not to be found in our bones, but in our very spirit, our selves, our personhood. Perhaps this is what on an earthly level Paul referred to as the spiritual body!

The Christian Faith through the ages has always affirmed that Jesus Christ was fully human–with bones! And fully divine. It seems to me that all this talk, all these books and films merely validate the one Christian belief, that Jesus was indeed a man. One scholar who commented upon the discovery of bones purported to be those of Jesus, announced with a note of joy that up until now we have had no tangible evidence that Jesus ever existed, but that now we have such proof. And, as Christians have been saying for centuries that Jesus was a man.

But we believe not, "just" a man, for we believe in his identity as God. Prior to Jesus' death and resurrection, his followers found his divinity difficult, if not impossible to grasp. It was Jesus appearance to his disciples after his resurrection which launched their belief that in some sense Jesus is God. His divinity remains foolishness to those who have not encountered the resurrected Christ.

The Gospel of John reports that when Mary Magdalene encountered the risen Christ she was kept from any physical contact, because his presence before her was not physical in the sense of flesh and bones. Bones restored to life were not needed for her faith, it would appear. Apparently a bit contrary to this affirmation of a resurrection which is spiritual, are the encounters which John tells in the paragraphs following his relating of Mary's experience. Here Jesus invites the disciples to see his hands and his side, areas which would show evidence of his crucifixion, and where Thomas declares that he would not believe until he both sees and touches the evidence of Jesus death in his hands and side. This Jesus permits him to experience. This remains a mystery, but the reply of Jesus stands: "Have you believed because you have seen me? Blessed are those who have not seen and yet have come to believe." (John 20:29 NRSV)

So, the bones aren't necessary. They can be found in whatever ossuary may indeed hold them. And the assaults from a ratings-crazed press and skeptical scholars–"sticks and stones"–can't hurt the true essence of Christian belief of those who have met the Risen Christ!

–April 2007

"THE STRIFE IS O'ER"

The execution of Jesus Christ; on the Cross was a cosmic 9-11. We believe that Jesus was in some sense God among us. When the terrorizing power of sin and death attempted to destroy God, the world experienced a catastrophic event comparable to 9-11 on a cosmic level.

The resurrection of Jesus Christ is God's decisive response to this cosmic 9-11 tragedy. Not with matching violence, as we did, but with the sheer power of love, God removed the terror of death and won the decisive victory over sin and evil, violence and death.

> Thus we sing:
> The strife is o'er–the battle done,
> The victory of life is won;
> The song of triumph has begun:
> Alleluia!

Instead of the massive lethal violence we used to "shock and awe" the perpetrators of our 9-ll, God brought to the world shock and awe in the quiet of Easter morning when the risen Christ appeared to his own–a powerful sign of God's victory over sin and evil.

> The pow'rs of death have done their worst,
> But Christ their legions hath dispersed;
> Let shouts of holy joy outburst:
> Alleluia

–April 17, 2007

PRONOUNCING "SHIBBOLETH"

It's happened again. Another anger crazed young male with a gun, killing thirty-two in a violent rampage on the campus of Virginia Tech in Blacksburg, Virginia. April 16, 2007–another day of infamy. What is going so very wrong in our society? Everyone seems to want to know the motive, as if this will make it all right, once we know why. I don't think so. There is no motive to balance the books on this most horrific killing in our history.

One of our local television news reporters was on the street interviewing people to get their reaction to the event, especially in regard to the availability of guns. Yesterday, I am sure, was a day when the so called gun lobby was on high alert, ready to "shoot down" anyone who might have entertained the notion that the killing in Blacksburg points to the need to do away with hand guns. One such gun enthusiast found on Main Street alleged that the police are not capable of giving us full protection, which necessitates the need for each of us to be ready to protect himself–with a gun, of course. By the way, he qualified for a pet peeve of mine. He spoke on camera wearing dark sun glasses. Others, I am sure repeated the gun lovers shibboleth–on camera and off–*It's not guns that kill people, people kill people.*

Think how different the scenario in Virginia would have been had the crazed individual, been reduced to using a baseball bat, or a kitchen knife. Many of the thirty-two families involved would not be grieving today, I am convinced. Forced to attack at close range, he would have been over-powered long before the death toll hit thirty-two.

Furthermore, I can't begin to imagine the lethal chaos which would have ensued if "Mr. Sunglasses on Main Street," with his particular gun lovers shibboleth. had his way. Can you imagine a university classroom in which each student carried a gun!

No, I believe that those who pronounce either of these gun lover shibboleths betray a point of view alien to the best interests of society. The word, *shibboleth* comes from a procedure used at a security check point in the days of the Judges of Israel (somewhere around 1100 years before the New Testament) At that time the Ephraimites were trying to infiltrate the forces of Gilead. Those who could not pronounce *shibboleth* properly were deemed to be Ephraimites and were therefore rejected.(Judges 12:5,6)

For the security of our society, in my opinion, those who use the shibboleths of the gun lobby pose a threat we need to take seriously. At the very least I would suggest we take off our dark sunglasses before we pronounce negative judgement on the possible restriction of firearms. A little more sunlight on the subject might indeed help us all.

–April 30, 2007

RELEVANCE AT THE COST OF REVERENCE

Mission Men is the title of an article in *Christian Century* (April 3, 2007), which is a response by Lilian Daniel, a UCC clergy person, to a new book by David Murrow, *Why Men Hate Going to Church.* She writes. "So what makes a church feminine? Morrow's answer comes from gender stereotypes as old as the hills, but freshly attuned to the pop culture of our day." Murrow's contention is that real men with adequate testosterone find the church boring with its preponderance of feminine activities and atmosphere and its absence of stimuli appealing to men. "Murrow worries that a female-dominated church has turned Jesus into that wonderful man who appeals only to the ladies. A chick-flick atmosphere prevails on Sunday mornings, complete with flowers, ferns and soft music, all geared toward women's desires for safety, security and harmonious relationships." Just not relevant to what men want, apparently.

Some years ago the Board of Christian Education, with a similar desire to appeal to modern-day youth in our culture, published two youth magazines, one for junior highs and another for high schoolers. There were articles extolling the normal activities of church kids, who were involved in sports and other areas life just like other kids. The message, it seemed to me, was that you don't have to be different from other kids to be a Christian. Another attempt to make the Christian message relevant.

These days another focus of the urge to be relevant is upon the music used in church worship. Traditional hymns of the church and the use of an organ have been relegated to the irrelevant and boring by many who choose the music and the instrument of the youth culture in an attempt to relate to today's youth. Again the message, it seems to me, is: *Come to our church where the music is no different from what fills your ears all week long.*

To be sure, these and other efforts to bring and keep people in the church, are well intentioned as methods of evangelism–presenting the Gospel to those who have somehow missed its message. But when, for the sake of appealing to new people, we dilute the message of the Gospel, might we be sacrificing Christian reverence for the holiness of God upon the altar of relevance?

This sort of relevance which influences the way some present the Christian Faith is set aside when one ponders the meaning of Jesus' words: "If any want to become my followers, let them deny themselves and take up their cross and follow me." (Mark 8:34 NRSV) Hear the way *The Message* concludes this teaching of Jesus: "If any of you are embarrassed over me and the way I'm leading you when you get around your fickle and unfocused friends, know that you'll be an even greater embarrassment to the Son of Man when he arrives in all the splendor of God, his Father with an army of holy angels."(Mark 8:38 Eugene, eterson, The Message)

The Christian Way is a yearned-for alternative to the ways of the world. A world desperately seeking peace while continuing to wage war and to engage in horrific violence needs to meet the Prince of peace through Christian women and men of peace. The hungry and the hurting need to be fed and healed through the love of God channeled through Christ's people who love and care. The oppressed and violated look for God's justice and must find it through the efforts of Christ's followers. And all people drift toward chaos until they reconnect with the Holy. Seeking to address these yearnings is the relevance which Christ asks of us.

–May 1, 2007

THIS IS THE ONE

In the 1940s Presbyterian young people were quite often organized into *Westminster Fellowships.* Among the resources which the national church provided to such youth groups was the *Westminster Fellowship Hymn.* This we sang lustily to the old Welsh hymn tune, CWM RHONDDA. One phrase in the first stanza was: *Youth at work are bringing God's own Glory to the earth from heaven above.* In the waning days of Westminster Fellowship, some astute Presbyterian interpreters of the Christian Faith turned a critical ear to these words. They challenged the theology of the hymn, saying that God is already in the world, and that God's presence in human life is not dependent upon *our* bringing God anywhere.

If they thought about it, I don't suppose the hymn writers would have resisted the clarification which the theological detractors brought to the matter. But on a deeper level, I wonder if the words in question betray a typical American attitude in the 1940's and today as well. We sang those words during the period of time when it was the mission of this nation to rid the world of Nazism and Japanese imperialism. Perhaps we Christians today have a bit of that same Messianic complex. We assume that it is up to Christians to feed the hungry, to free the oppressed, and to bring, justice to a hurting world. We who were steeped in the optimism of the 1940 s still sing in effect, *We are at work bringing God's redemption to our world.*

Ultimately it is God who redeems. Our task is to identify those points in the contemporary scene at which God's redemptive hand is at work, to bear witness to God's action, and to answer God's call to join in such redemptive effort where possible. God's glory is to bd all around us. We need the eyes of faith to see it, and the courage to name it to the world which is blind to the wondrous works of God. We need the humility to acknowledge the fact that the redeeming work of God is not confined to what the church and Christians do. God works through people of all faiths and those with no formal religious affiliation. God works through so called secular institutions as well, and we need to affirm that.

Sometime in the 1960s a certain Christian Campus ministry used a slogan reminiscent of the Westminster Fellowship Hymn, *Bringing Christ to the Campus.* Others of us responded with the same corrective which had been applied to the Westminster Fellowship Hymn: *He is already here.* We saw in the slogan an arrogance borne out of the belief that it was their job to introduce Christ, the Savior to a lost and sinful campus. The implication here was that if anything good and Godly is to be done, Christians in the church must do it–through their kind of church at that.

As we go into the world, or onto the university campus, we go, not *bringing* Christ, but as Christ's ambassadors, *bearing witness* to Christ's presence not only in the church, but in the world beyond the church. We are to be like John the Baptist who said, "I am not the Messiah. . (and then turning to Jesus). . . Here is the Lamb of God who takes away the sin of the world." (John 1:20, 29) Eugene Peterson puts it this way: *John pointed him out and called, "This is the One!"* (John 1:29 The Message) Our function is like John's, to point to the Christ wherever we see him and to proclaim. *Here is God's redemption at work in the world!*

–June 12, 2007

WHO DO YOU TALK TO?

After reading a letter to the editor from Joel Biggers, a United Methodist pastor and a friend, I got to thinking about who it is we ought to talk to. Joel makes it clear when he writes. "So I write this letter for seekers, Christians, Muslims, Hindus, Buddhists, agnostics and atheists who may wonder if conservative Christians are the only ones who exist." The letter has to do with the creationist argument and pointed to the creation museum in Kentucky sponsored by Biblical literalists to "protect Biblical literalism." He essentially said that not all Christians are creationists, and that many believe that science points us to the answers to questions of how the physical world has come about. He pointed out that this scientific approach need not negate; the truth of the Bible. "You can be a Christian and believe the theory of evolution." He writes.

When I first read Joel's letter I said to myself, *Listen, you literalists, this letter contains the truth you need to correct your misguided theology.* Then I thought better of it, because I realized that those who are set in their ways will not listen. Instead they will fight and call Joel an evil unbeliever. That's the way it was during the former battle over the virgin birth. Those who did not believe in the virgin birth, or who, at the very least, said it doesn't matter, were judged un-Christian by the fundamentalists at the time. There seems to be a listing of key issues over which to fight and by which to judge who's in and who's outside the true faith. Bodily resurrection and the divinity of Jesus are on that list of litmus tests these days. I might be a bit cynical, but it seems to me that there are those rigid ones who simply enjoy a good fight with those who are less rigid in their beliefs. And judging by the fact that millions have been collected to put up the creation museum in Kentucky, there are many who are willing to finance a fight against the infidels, So better not write letters to such rigid ones!

As Joel Biggers perceives, some of the ones whose minds may be more pliable are to be found among seekers and agnostics–and I would add-- those who have been turned off by rigid insensitivity in churches with which they have had previous contact. These are the ones we must talk to. We must tell them that our thoughts are much closer to theirs than they have been led to understand. This is what Joel has done, but the task has just begun.

–June 2007

NOAH AND THE WHALE

A recurring and disconcerting news story which frequents newspapers these days is the reporting of declining membership numbers in mainline denominations. Often such articles cite the membership growth of so-called "evangelical" churches as a significant contrast. This usually puts main-liners' noses out of joint. At this point, a flurry of analyses usually take place. Some make the claim that members are leaving the mainline churches and are joining the more conservative churches. Frequently, the reason given for this movement is that the mainline churches have deserted the traditional Biblical faith for modern scientific theories, and that people want a Bible-believing church. Oddly, other analysts say the opposite, claiming that many contemporary Americans have been turned off by churches which talk about the Bible in traditional terms, without regard for modern-day scientific knowledge or current social issues. These folk, many of whom are young adults, simply drop out of church, considering it asleep and irrelevant.

Much to my chagrin, I have to admit that there is truth in the rationale underlying both of these movements. In pondering these seemingly contradictory reactions to today's churches, I have come to see that we have failed to educate our people over the years, particularly in biblical interpretation and understanding. In 1953 when I was a young pastor, a nearby congregation employed a seminary graduate who unwisely enjoyed shocking his congregation with the new ideas he had learned in seminary. When he proudly announced that there was no such person as Noah and no such event as the flood, requiring no such thing as an ark, he was met with hostile opposition from his congregation. His was a blatant failure as a Christian educator. Sadly, he was not alone. Most newly trained seminary grads simply didn't bring up the matter and left their members to continue to hold to literal interpretations of the Bible with which they were familiar. At about that same time the Revised Standard Version of the Bible came out and certain passages which had read "virgin" in the King James Bible, read "young woman" in the RSV. This, of course, fed the fires of controversy over the belief in the virgin birth. When met with the old "saw," "If the King James Version was good enough for God, it's good enough for me." many mainline ministers laughed. They knew better, but failed to educate their congregations adequately in the development of the Bible. The truth of the matter is either version is good enough for God!

We simply have not helped people to grow in their understanding in such a way that the advances in scientific knowledge do not pose a threat to faith. And so the science vs. religion battle of the 1920 s has reignited in our time with mainline churches acknowledging the insights of evolution and the "evangelical" churches preaching creationism. One more reason for people who have not been led beyond blind literalism to transfer to churches which "believe in the Bible."

At the same time, our failure to educate has made it appear to many that the mainline churches, just like the conservative ones, hold to a literal view of the Bible with it's pre-scientific world view. And so they drop out, relegating the church to the scrap heap of history.

But there's hope. And hope lies in earnest education by which one can be helped to embrace both science and religion, and by which one can discern the Word of God beneath human-bound words of the Bible. During my seminary years a young man transferred to our seminary from a very conservative Bible institute where, he complained, he had been involved in a semester-long project in which he was asked to prove that a whale could have indeed swallowed a man who, indeed could have survived as Jonah was purported to have done. In our seminary he was freed of the obligation to accept the Bible literally, and given the opportunity to be taught to probe beneath the ancient words of the Bible to uncover the timeless truths of God.

Dare we do less in the educational enterprise of the mainline churches? So that the message of Noah is that of God's saving grace, and the significance of the whale is God's call to mission!

–July 2007

I'LL PRAY FOR YOU, BROTHER

Some years ago when I was pastor of St. Andrew Church a previously active member came in to my office to tell me that he was leaving St. Andrew Church. It was never easy for me when I realized that someone had left the congregation either to join another church or for none at all. Rarely did any of these drop-outs come in to talk about their impending termination, as did this particular elder sitting before me. He told me of having found a new and deeper spiritual experience elsewhere, and topped this declaration off with these stinging words: "You're just not there yet, Paul. Someday, hopefully you will be." I don't know whether he did or not, but his words were tantamount to telling me, "I'll pray for you, brother."

Lately I have discovered that there is a group of ministers and elders in our presbytery who meet by telephone conference call, "to pray for the presbytery." On the one hand it is perfectly appropriate to pray for the presbytery. We do that each time a meeting of the presbytery is opened, and sometimes during the sessions when some a particular matter seems to call for prayer. But for a small group from within the larger membership to comes together to pray "for the rest of us" so to speak, my suspicions are raised and I feel a resurgence of that old sting, I felt one day in my office in St. Andrew. I can't help but feel that there is a hidden agenda which could be termed, "I'll pray for you, brother." The mere fact that such suspicions surface, gives evidence of the precarious divide which has been cleft among us in Yellowstone Presbytery.

At a time when there is effort needed to bring unity to the broken fellowship of the presbytery, the last thing we need is for one bunch of us to self righteously to pray for others of us who "aren't there yet."

I hope my suspicions are ill-founded.

WRY BREAD.....food for thought with a wry twist
–September 2007

YOU CAN TELL A LOT ABOUT A PERSON from. . . .

You can tell a lot about a person from his or her particular approach to yard maintenance. Some people who dress "just so" keep their lawns trimmed very neatly. On the other hand, straggly grass and trees needing pruning may indicate a very laid-back neighbor, or if that same yard has lots of recreation equipment like boats and four-wheelers strewn around, the straggly lawn tells you that this home owner would much rather be out on the lakes and streams. Of course the longer you observe a yard, the more you pick up about its keeper. I once had a neighbor whom I did not know very well, but over time I noticed some things about his approach to yard care. We both had some very difficult strips along the road to care for because of very rocky ground which seemed to produce only ugly weeds. Unsightly, yes, but now his was even worse. Everything is a barren yellow/brown, and nothing at all will grow along his right-of-way. He had spread something on the ground which not only killed the weeds but deadened the soil for years to come. At first there were a number of nice trees in his yard. Not anymore. When the apple trees got fire blight, he cut them down. The cottonwoods were messy and filled his yard with twigs and leaves, until he had them removed. It appears to me that my neighbor's approach to problems was a "cut and slash" method. *If it bothers you, kill it!*

I could be wrong, and possibly quite unfair, for after all I didn't really know him very well and I realize my own yard leaves something to be desired. However. . . .

You can tell a lot about a person from his or her personalized license plate. People often like to display their particular interests, such as *SKI-DADDY,* or *QUILTER.* Some folks even give a Scripture verse like *JN 3:16.* That one is ok, because I know what it says, but when it is a verse I don't know, it is a lot of trouble to jot it down, find a Bible, and see what the verse says, while driving.

Back to my neighbor, the one who solves yard problems by removing the whole tree. His license plate reads *B52 PLT.* Makes you wonder.

–September 2007

A WORK IN PROGRESS

Some personal theological reflections

There is a major development going on in my theological thinking. Rereading Walter Wink's *The Powers that Be* has given me some insights into my thinking to date. He talks of four world views, and suggests that the Materialistic world view has been pervasive in our science-minded culture, and I find it to be most operative in my thinking and theology.

This materialistic world view, unlike others before it, does not allow for a spiritual or divine reality. All truth is limited to the material which is discernible through the five senses, and thus verifiable. In an extreme version of the, Materialistic world view, God and anything spiritual is not objectively real, but is conjured up in the minds of people for one reason or another. God is a figment of one's imagination to serve one's own purposes. For example, according to this view, ideas of an afterlife are invented to help one face death.

When one has this world view, it is difficult if not impossible to include the Christian concept of God and God's action in one's view of reality. This divine dimension is beyond the limits of the physical reality in the materialist's world view and accessible by faith, not by sight. Faith at worst is wishful imagination, but to the Christian, faith is a gift of God, God's own revelation, rather than a result of a person's own effort.

The question of how God acts in the material world, or whether God does act and the related question of prayer present a struggle in thinking for the Christian who has been schooled in the rational, scientific, materialist world view. From a strictly materialist view there is no room for God to act in the physical and historical development of reality. Events proceed according to the laws of nature and the logical progression of historical circumstances. Cancer cells are diminished by radiation or chemotherapy, not by supposed divine intervention. Earthquakes destroy villages and human lives because of the shifting of plates beneath the surface of the earth, which no "hand of God" could change. The cause of Hurricane Katrina is to be found in the particular meteorological factors leading up to it, not in the wrathful action of a God upset with human behavior. If a critical bolt holding in place the wing of an airline is coming loose, no amount of prayer will tighten it.

But nevertheless Christians believe they are invited by God to pray for favorable outcomes for themselves and for others. And Christians with strong evidence from the experience of God's people in the Bible believe that God leads them–at least occasionally–safely through life's ups and downs. Every so often one hears of someone who for one reason or another missed or decided not to board a certain flight, only to find that their intended flight crashed, killing all on board. And that particular person attributes his or her well-being to God's protective action. What the Christian calls providence, the materialist calls coincidence.. When the rationalist says, "That's just how things work out," some Christians affirm, "The will of God."

Other Christians with a materialist world view are not so sure, a skepticism which echoed my thinking most of the time until lately. I did not believe that God would intervene in the rationally ordered progression of nature or the working out of history. And yet one prays for safety and success of one sort or anoher. How can one have it both ways? How can a materialist pray, if at all?

Many years ago I led a study of Harold Kushner's *Why Do Bad Things Happen to Good People.* In seeking to answer this question, Kushner sets God's love, power and justice over and against each other and concludes that for God to be both all loving and just, God cannot be all-powerful. For an all-powerful God to love everyone, and yet for not everyone to be healed, God's justice would be lacking. If God is all loving and just, he must not be all-powerful. Therefore our prayers for healing will not necessarily bring about desired results. So what is the benefit of one's praying. Kushner's answer is that our prayers help us to face whatever circumstances come our way including the "bad things." Many of us in that study group came away frustrated with so weak a definition of prayer. My materialist-bound theology began to give way when I concluded that in some mysterious way, one's prayer, together with the prayers of others and joined with God's loving will, do in fact make a difference.

As it was becoming clear that we were entering what now is called the *Postmodern Age,* the absolute truth of the materialistic-rational world view has shown some cracks. The *New Physics* provided some "loop holes." It was appearing that the laws of Newtonian Physics governed only a segment of the universe, and that there might be reality beyond what we knew as our own. The Heisenberg principle of randomness opened up reality, it seemed to me, for room for what had been considered supernatural intervention, At any rate things weren't so concrete anymore.

Subsequently I became fascinated with the philosophy of Alfred North Whitehead and the resulting Process Theology of John Cobb and others. My abbreviated "take" on what they were saying was that God is involved in every thing and in every event, seeking to bring about God's will and intention in the midst of other opposing forces and influences. This thinking came as an answer to my question of how to integrate belief in an acting God in a materialist world-view. Theologically I affirmed the ultimate accomplishment of God's will, even though in the short term, evil and sin still, to some extent, have sway. This brought back one of the theories of the Atonement which appealed to me in my seminary reading of Gustav Aulen's interpretation of the idea of *Christus Victor,* which proclaims that in the resurrection Christ has overcome the powers of evil, even though in the meantime they are still at work opposing God. The decisive battle has been won by God, but minor skirmishes will still continue until the end.

Finally in the last few weeks a second reading of Walter Wink's *The Powers that Be* has moved me further in my attempt to integrate the material and the divine. Wink helped me to define my earlier position through his description of what he calls *The Theological World View.* According to this view there is a material realm, discernible scientifically through the five senses, and a supernatural realm known by faith. In its extreme form these two realities, while both are valid, are entirely separate and do not integrate. The late Willem Zurrdeeg, a seminary professor of mine, used the term *Logic Tight Compartmentalization* to describe the way in which some people hold conflicting views from science and religion at the same time without attempting any integration.

Walter Wink goes on to describe an emerging world view which I find very helpful in moving my thinking forward to accept a more vigorous action of God and a more efficacious view of prayer. He calls this new view *An Integral Worldview.* "The integral view of reality sees everything as having an outer and an inner aspect. . .(affirming) spirit as the core of every created thing. But, inextricably related to an outer form or physical manifestation." (Walter Wink, The Powers that Be, pp.19-20, Doubleday - A Galilee Book 1998)

For me this view now puts God within the material and historical world, and appropriately capable of acting in this realm. One's prayer does not then ask for what can't be done! Reality can now be experienced in a multi-dimensional way, no longer flat and limited to sense perception, but now through prayerful contemplation one can begin to connect with the inner core of things.

This is a new way of thinking and one which does not easily replace the old materialistic view, taught and held fast these many years. But this is a work in progress which holds real potential for new spiritual insight and depth in my life.

–December 24, 2007

DANGER–THIN ICE

Apparently Christmas can be a troublesome time for some who call themselves atheists or humanists. I believe that those who take this intellectual position have built walls of cold rationalism–walls of ice--around the their own mental capacities in such a way as to permit no intrusion of any thoughts or feelings which originate beyond the strictly rational human world in which they live. Christmas by its true definition comes from beyond such walls and so I would think it to be indeed troublesome for those who have constructed such a walled citadel around themselves. There is a sense in which Christmas can be dangerous for them as well as troublesome, for the meaning of Christmas, especially as it is communicated through the arts, has the power to permeate such walls, melting them with the warmth of Divine love.

During this season of Christmas a group of Harvard students have been struggling to find a way around the festivities of Christmas. On Sunday morning, December 23rd, National Public Radio reported on a discussion an atheist/humanist association at that prestigious university was having over the question of whether or not they could sing Christmas carols. This spirited debate was led by the university atheist chaplain, apparently a former practicing Jew. The hardliners in the group proclaimed that for them singing Christmas carols would be a betrayal of their atheist position, because through singing the familiar carols they would be admitting to a religious point of view, contrary to their atheist/humanist position which does not permit them to believe in a higher power, a belief which the Christmas carols certainly proclaim.

The soft line approach to this problem, which by the way was held be the atheist chaplain who admitted that he still enjoys lighting his Menorah, begged for some singing of the carols out of a nostalgic celebration of past Christmases. Students taking the soft line wanted to be able to sing carols without giving up their atheist position. There seemed to be variations in this position, some saying that one would need to change the words to omit any religious references, others seeming to say that one didn't have to believe the religious stuff when singing the carols. One of the most telling thoughts expressed in this discussion was that without singing this music there was something missing.

For some with this humanist philosophy there seems to be a thinning of the atheist wall which shuts out anything beyond this world. There seems to be a yearning for the warm feelings, feelings which do not emanate from the cold human rationalist mind inside the wall. Danger! Thin ice. The ice house constructed by humanists unwilling to see beyond the rational may begin to melt under the warmth of the singing of Christmas carols!

Coincidentally, a few hours after hearing this discussion on NPR I stood in worship with other Christians and uttered these words of the Confession of 1967: *"God's sovereign love is a mystery beyond the reach of the human mind."*

Yes, God's love does indeed break through the walls we build around ourselves. God's love is most powerful in the sending of God's Son, Jesus Christ into the world to save us from ourselves–*Emmanuel*–God coming through the walls we build to try to keep out divine intervention.

The radiant warmth of God's love is indeed a danger to the thin ice of the walls constructed by an atheist/humanist mind set–or by those of us who don't allow God to be very much of an influence in our materialistic lives. May Christmas melt the walls of ice we have built as well!

— December 24, 2007

–Epiphany 2008

"AND LO! THE EASTERN SAGES. . . ."

In 1736 Charles Coffin wrote these words which have become a part of the poetry of Epiphany: *"And lo! the Eastern sages stand to read in heaven the Lord's command."* The command according to Matthew is to pay homage to the King of the Jews. (Mt 2:2), despite the fact that these men were not Jews. Matthew's message is that people from outside the faith boundaries of Judaism were commanded by God to pay homage to Jesus Christ. And certain Eastern sages did just that.

This proclamation of Matthew flies in the face of the parochial message in our current culture. We are told today that only Christians should pay homage to Christ. And that other people have other religious beliefs, which are to be held as equal to the beliefs Christians hold. Following this secular prohibition, statues of the sages from the East and other regular participants in the Christmas Creche are said not to belong on the Courthouse lawn at Christmas time.

Curiously, the Eastern Sages represent the people in the world "out there" beyond the boundaries of the faith. And so it is, the eastern sages who by definition ought to be most at home on the courthouse lawn, for these are the secular thinkers, who by custom and law belong on tax-supported property.

But, wait a minute, that is exactly where the star led these folk. When they got there the King was missing and so they stepped inside to ask the officials in the courthouse where the child king was and

Herod told them where the King was to be found. And Herod became insanely worried that the king whom the sages sought would take away his power.

Maybe that's why the sages and all the other manger statues have been driven from "Herod's" front lawn. It's a stretch–but think about it.

WRY BREAD...Food for thought with a wry twist
–January 2008

THE JIG IS UP!

Just so that we don't become too complacent, a recent calculation presented to a national meeting of astronomers in Austin Texas will put an end to any assumptions that we might be eternal. We are told that the end is coming and fast–at a rate of one hundred and fifty miles per second. That's quite fast. To put this in perspective–of sorts–we could compare this speed to going the 140 miles from Bozeman to Billings in just under a second. That means you could go to the Rimrock Mall, buy a coveted item, and be back in Bozeman in less that ten minutes–that is if they have the item. So, it's the good life–but temporary. The jig is up. It is only a matter of time.

What is it that is coming at us at such a rate, you might ask. It is a huge cloud of gas, many times the size of our sun. When this collides with our galaxy the explosion will be enormous, so much so that new stars will be formed, presumably to replace the planet we presently occupy.

None of our usual safe-guards will be able to give us much help, not even the very latest military hardware upon which we are accustomed to depend for security purposes. Of course we don't know for sure. National security requires that any development of such a deterrent will be held as top secret, and we will have to trust our Defense Department to be ready when the time comes. But it is coming–at a speed of one hundred fifty miles per second.

Short of dependence upon the federal government, one is tempted to turn to more personal measures. No doubt there will be those opposing any form of gun control, who will take comfort in our constitutional right to possess firearms, which will enable each homeowner to be ready with handguns and other weapons when this catastrophe comes upon us. And it is coming! At a rate of one hundred fifty miles per second. It is indeed on the way.

Global warming is nothing compared to what is in store for our planet, giving a rather far- reaching excuse to those nay-sayers who don't believe in such environmental talk. For after all total extinction of all species is coming at one hundred fifty miles per second. So why not keep the lights on and do away with the wolves as well.

Well, what should we do? Go to church? A lot of people did right after 9-11. But one hundred fifty miles per second. That's a lot faster than anything the church ever does. Nah! This is bigger than God. And further away as well. The astronomers tell us that the lethal cloud is forty-seven quadrillion miles away. Wait a minute. Do the math. It will take forty million years for IT to get here. What a relief. That will give the Defense Department time. . . and the church as well. Or will it? One hundred fifty miles per second. The jig is up–we are not eternal after all.

–February 15, 2008

SING US THE OLD SONG

A "long time ago" Pete Seeger wrote a protest song which became very popular in the 1960s. Among its memorable lines two have come to mind today after another school slaughter with firearms–this time in a lecture hall at Northern Illinois University. If that ill fated hall could remember, the strains of Pete Seeger's *Where have all the flowers gone?* might still be heard. But instead, the sound of repeated gunfire amid chaotic screams filled the hall as a lone gunman appeared on stage and fired randomly into the audience using both the shotgun and the handguns which he had brought with him. Six people were killed, fifteen others were injured.

Oh, "When will *we* ever learn?" Isn't it time for us as a nation to take courageous and radical steps to ban the private use of handguns and severely to regulate the private use of other firearms? Recently the District of Columbia took such an action. However fifty-five senators and two hundred and fifty representatives have objected and are urging the Supreme Court to strike down this ban on constitutional grounds. Sadly, Montana's delegation in both Houses are supporting this challenge to D.C.'s prudent action. And Montana, through its Attorney General, has joined thirty other states in support of private handgun ownership.

Those who oppose a ban on handguns quote the Second Amendment of the U.S. Constitution: "A well-regulated militia, being necessary to the security of a free state, the rights of the people to keep and bear arms shall not be infringed." It would appear that this amendment for some in the gun lobby has attained near divine status. One of the current contenders for President was heard to claim that the second amendment, he believes, is as sacred as the first amendment which grants free speech. Tell that to the six families who are mourning grievously today. Free to speak and free to kill! Oh, "When will *we* ever learn?"

Might we not take a critical look at the second amendment, conceived in an 18th Century agrarian society, now that we live in the urban sprawl of the 21st Century? If we are not willing to consider amending the amendment, then let's take a long a hard look at the word *well-regulated* in the second amendment.

Where have all the young *ones* gone?

Long time ago....When will *we* ever learn?

–March 2008

THE SILLY SEASON

As the campaign rhetoric heats up between the two contending Democratic presidential hopefuls, the media pundits are beginning to refer to this period of time as *The Silly Season.* While the word *silly* tends to marginalize what is being said, I would like to challenge one silly idea which the two campaigns have brought to light: that people in churches ought to agree with what their preachers say from the pulpit, or to put it the other way around, that preachers ought to preach only what their congregations will agree with. The media has been playing and replaying snippets of what the Rev. Jeremiah Wright, long time pastor of Senator Obama's congregation, said regarding the shortcomings of the United States in matters of justice and peace. The basic implication set forth by those who uncovered these sermons is that if Wright said it, Obama must think the same way. This exposes the silly idea that preachers and their congregations always agree on everything the preacher says in his sermons. Using this silly assumption, Obama is judged guilty by association. Further exposing this silly idea, many pundits, political candidates, and people on the street who have been interviewed on the subject have piously declared that "if my preacher, rabbi, or priest said that, I'd leave his church." and under their breath they say "and Obama certainly should have left that church, if he didn't agree with what Wright said."

So there you have it! According to this definition of preaching, sermons ought to consist only of ideas and view points which are already known and agreed upon by the congregations they address. And if, by chance, one should hear something disagreeable, the only honorable thing to do is to leave that church. According to this silly definition, any preacher foolish enough to be worth his salt and who is courageously proclaiming the Word of God, will have a pile of departure letters on his or her desk most Monday mornings.

Thus the advice from this silly season is: *If you don't like what you hear from your preacher, leave. If you want to remain as their preacher, tell them what they want to hear, and what they already think.*

'Tis the silly season, indeed.

–April 8, 2008

(or if you like) WRIGHT IS WRONG

Today, Dr. Jeremiah Wright, retired pastor of the Trinity United Church of Christ in Chicago, is speaking to the National Press Club in Washington D.C. It is thus apparent that he has accepted this coveted opportunity, and at a time when some of his former words are still being used to jeopardize the campaign opportunity and at a time when some of his former words are still being used to jeopardise the campaign of Senator Barack Obama for the Democratic nomination for the presidency, at a time when any further media attention he garners may very well continue to have a negative effect upon Obama's chances.

Presidential primary competition has turned ugly. Hillary has Bill. Barack has Jeremiah. While the Clinton campaign can muzzle Bill, the Obama Campaign apparently cannot muzzle Jeremiah Wright–nor can they muzzle the press which has been goading Wright on for the benefit of its own ratings-- while both the Clinton and McCain campaigns look on with glee.

In my opinion, three of the lower forms of public expression are evident in this Wright affair, each of which has the potential of derailing Obama's quest for the presidency.

(1) *Attacking on the basis of guilt by association.* In the 1950s many honorable Americans were condemned to obscurity or worse because of having been in the same room with a Communist at some earlier time in their lives. Now the public has been urged

to conclude that because Obama sat in a church listening to Jeremiah Wright, Barack Obama is unfit for the presidency.

(2) *Placing profit ahead of decency and fairness.* When the media picked up the questionable portions of Wright's sermons and challenged Barack Obama with them, broadcasting this over and over to the public, its love for financial bottom line far outweighed any judgment for decency and fairness, I believe.

(3) *Selling the greater good in the service of self aggrandizement.* This, I believe, has led Jeremiah Wright to use whatever public platform has opened up to him in order to defend himself and to widen the audience for his viewpoints. Or, perhaps to put it more mildly, at least it can be said that Wright did not turn down such self-serving opportunities in the interest of the greater good--fairness or support to his parishioner, Barack Obama.

While Jeremiah Wright ought to have the right to preach prophetically, as indeed every Christian preacher ought to be so encouraged, I believe his intrusion into the national political arena in collusion with the media is not right. In what has happened *since* the original story first broke, I believe Wright is wrong!

–December 28, 2008

THE SECOND DAY OF CHRISTMAS

(a journal entry which begs for a sequel)

On the second day of Christmas 2008, instead of a partridge in a pear tree, Israeli bombers appeared in the sky over the Gaza strip and dropped one hundred tons of bombs killing two hundred seventy-five persons and wounding at least six hundred more. Those who sent the bombs said it was in retaliation for mortar attacks upon Israel. The mortar attacks which followed were called by those who lobbed them a reprisal for the bombings. Whatever it is called, *dead* is *dead.* And so the spiral of violence continues.

On the second day of Christmas when Christian people here and there lounged in their homes re-reading their Christmas cards, warplanes (most likely-American made) dumped terror onto the streets of Gaza City. The message on many of the cards which people were reading was *Peace on Earth.*

On the second day of Christmas we have been announcing the coming to earth of the Prince of Peace–on the second day of Christmas 2008, when 200,000 pounds of airborne bombs were being flung to earth intended to kill people and to destroy their city, at a time when many were wishing each other."Merry Christmas and Peace on Earth!"

On the second day of Christmas, what are we to think? Fifty-six years ago I was ordained to preach the Good news of Jesus Christ in a world needing the message of the Prince of Peace. In fact, one of my motivations for going into the ordained ministry was to further the realization of peace in the world. During the time since my ordination our nation has been engaged in a seemingly endless progression of wars: Korea, Viet Nam, Iraq, Afghanistan, and the all-pervasive War on Terror. Throughout much of this time the spiral of violence has been going back and forth in the Middle East. And each Advent Season I spoke of the romise of the Prince of Peace whom we joyfully and solemnly welcomed each Christmas.

What are we to think? In 1954, a few years after World War II, the World Council of Churches held its second assembly in Evanston, Illinois. As visitors to this most significant meeting of Christians from many countries of the world, Doris and I were aware of a difference of interpretation of the theme of the assembly, *Christ, the Hope of the World.* As Americans we saw in this theme an assurance that if we worked hard enough for peace we would realize world peace in our time. However, European Christians who had recently emerged from the shambles of World War II could not grasp such assurance. They interpreted the theme rather in eschatological terms–that our hope for peace would be realized at the end of time when Christ returns. We thought "How sad" that war had so damaged European hopes for the realization of peace in our world in our time, while our hope was for peace now.

Now, a half century later which has been filled with war and violence, I am not so sure but that the European interpretation might be the only viable one.

On the second day of Christmas, must we wait until the end of time to see the partridge come to the pear tree? While in the meantime the bombers of this world continue to fill the sky?

–January 2009

WHOSE LAND?

In the light of the current vicious and violent fight over land ownership in the Middle East I find the words of Gary Anderson, Old Testament professor at the University of Notre Dame, most disconcerting. "Christians must also insist that the promises of scripture are indeed inviolable and that Israel's attachment to this land is underwritten by God's providential decree." I don't think so. I believe that the Old Covenant has been abrogated by God in the sending of his Son, Jesus Christ, into the world to establish a New Covenant which God offers to all humanity, not just to a particular racial or ethnic group. God established a new covenant sealed in the blood of Jesus, crucified on the Cross. "This cup is the new covenant in my blood." (I Corinthians 11:25).

I believe that this new inclusive covenant offered to all people replaces the old exclusive covenant given to the Jews only.

To insist that the promises of Scripture are inviolable is, I think, to limit God. The words of Scripture are the written form of the thinking and belief of a particular human community in whose life God acted. No human thought or words can completely and perfectly capture the full truth of God and enshrine that truth in a certain time and place. The Sovereign God carries on God's redemptive work when, where and how God wills at any point it time. As a Christian I believe that there came a time when God's redemption of humanity was enacted in the life, death and resurrection of Jesus of Nazareth, in whom, we believe, God comes to earth to lovingly redeem God's creation. God redeeming work began in his promises to Abraham and reached ultimate fulfillment in

Jesus Christ. To try and hold God to the specifics of his promises to Abraham as interpreted by his people at the time is to reduce God to a mere actor on the stage of history, bound by the conventional thought of a certain age.

Whose land? As a Christian I sing with the Psalmist: *The earth is the Lord's and fullness thereof; the world and they that dwell therein.* (Psalm 24:1) And from Jesus I take heart: *Then he took a cup. . . he gave it to them, saying, "Drink from it, all of you."*

–February 2009

GOING WITH THE FLOW?

A friend recently sent me a copy of a meditation by Richard Rohr. The following portion of it caught my eye:

> *How can you read the Eight Beatitudes and the Sermon on the Mount and not believe Jesus was teaching nonviolence? It's impossible. . . (However) we didn't teach that. . . we weren't interested in changing this world. We have to go to our Mennonite and Amish and Quaker brothers and sisters who, thank God, retained the peace witness of the church.*
> --Richard Rohr

One such theologian puts it this way

> *Church history is a sad story. . . After the first three centuries when almost all Christians refused to participate in warfare, Christians repeatedly invented ways to justify violene.*
> –Ronald J. Sider

At the very core, justification of the use of violence, whether in warfare or in confronting an armed intruder at one's front door, amounts to some form of the statement *I must use violence to keep myself or my family from being killed.* To this assertion Sider declares that

> Jesus came announcing a new Way–the Kingdom of God, in which the people of God will emulate Jesus and the way of the cross. Jesus refused to use violence and instead approached his enemies with love. When we are stuck in the ways of the world we label this idealistic claim of Jesus as utopian and unrealistic. The cynic would say: *That's the way to get yourself killed.* Which is exactly what happened to Jesus. *"He submitted to Roman execution to reconcile his enemies."*
> (Sider)

This is the way of the Kingdom of God which Jesus came ushering in. We have a very difficult time accepting his announcement, much less living the new Way. It is the resurrection which validates Jesus' claim to be the New King. Again Sider declares: *"If as Christians claim, the grave could not hold Him, then his messianic kingdom has truly begun and the way of the cross is the way of the risen Sovereign of this whole glorious universe."* But is the way of the cross the way which those of us who call ourselves Christian are really following? Sadly, it is doubtful, given our track record over the centuries.

I am guessing that the majority of Montana state legislators would identify themselves as Christian. And yet there is in the current session of the legislature a bill to allow the use of handguns by individual householders when they or their families are lethally threatened. At this point there is some indication that this may pass into law. When we look at this situation through the eyes of the present world, we are quick to conclude that in Montana any legislator who votes against this bill will face the very real possibility of losing the next election.

There we are! To oppose the use of violence in one's own castle on Christian grounds could very well be the Way of the Cross! Suffering servanthood for the reconciliation of the world. To oppose U.S. military action in Iraq and elsewhere in the world is at least to be unpopular among one's neighbors, or more seriously to be labeled as un-American–a level of "crucifixion" either way. More outspoken and active opposition to U.S. involvement in war will put one at greater risk of persecution from patriotic supporters of the war. Out of a natural desire to get along with one's neighbors, many of us simply don't want to rock the boat with some form of stand against violence. So we go with the flow.

Furthermore, there are many American Christians, I think, who conclude that for an individual to refuse participation in warfare or any other manifestation of violence will make little difference in the overall drift of history. Some feel that there will always be wars and violence. We are tempted to conclude that violence and war are just part of our primitive human nature, and that whatever one does or doesn't do won't change anything. So what good is it to choose non-violence. This, I think, is the basis for a great deal of apathy when it comes to Christ's call to a non-violent life . It seems to be the nature of Americans to think that one can indeed fix things, but when that does not seem possible it is best to go with the flow.

It is precisely at this point that Jesus enters the life of the world to proclaim and embody a new way–the Kingdom of God, in which love replaces violence. He teaches us God's new way of love:

> "But I say to you love your enemies and pray for those who persecute you."
> (Matthew 5:44)

To do that, I can't any longer go with the flow. Jesus chose the cross instead of the "flow."

I ask myself. *Is it too strong a declaration to say to myself, that unless I choose the cross and forsake violence and war, I will be judged as less than faithful?* Again Jesus teaches:

> "If any want to become my followers, let them deny themselves and take up their cross daily and follow me."
> (Luke 9:23)

–March 3, 2009
(On the occasion of a Presbytery meeting.)

NOT TO DIVIDE, BUT TO UNITE

Jesus did not come that we might glorify ourselves and our own opinions but so that we might submit only to the glory of God. Jesus did not come to divide people from each other but to unite us. Jesus did not come that we might succumb to prideful dominating of others, but in humility to submit to God and to the loving community he calls us into in Christ. Jesus did not come for warfare and strife, party wrangling and hatred, but to bring reconciliation and peace. Jesus did not want us to tear apart the body of Christ but dwell with each other in love and respect despite our differences.

–March 2009

THE EMPEROR'S RULE IS ENDING. . . FINALLY

For sixteen centuries or so the assumption in the West has been that we are all Christian, or at least that we ought to be. But now the Emperor's Rule is ending. The shining medallion of the Christian faith is beginning to tarnish as more and more former "Christians" are tossing their lapel crosses into the trash. A report of the American Religious Idetification Survey has recently been carried in the popular press which indicates that in 1990, 15% of the population in the U.S. claim no religion at all, let alone owning up to a Christian identification. Add to that statistic, the finding that another 12% of Americans who, while they believe in a higher power, do not believe in a personal God as proclaimed by the Christian faith. When most major Christian denominations report declining membership and shrinking worship attendance, one does not need a survey to conclude that we are not really a "Christian nation" anymore, as some have assumed for a number of years.

Since Emperor Constantine the Great declared Christianity to be the official religion of the Roman Empire in the early fourth century, Rome's successors have established the Christian Church as the official religious affiliation of their people. Despite the separation of church and state in this country, the cultural bias has remained, holding that Christian faith and citizenship are somewhat synonymous, with the exception of small minorities of adherents to other religions such as Judaism.

This assumption of Christian majority and superiority has been debilitating. The confusion of loyalties to one's country and one's religion has kept the prophetic voice of the Church in some sense shackled. There has also been the tendency for patriotic Christians to claim that service to country is by definition obedience to Christ. "What's good for General Motors and the U.S. is good for Christ," might be the motto for such culture-Christians.

But the Emperor's Rule is ending. Now freed from religious Americanization, Christians can now say and do unpatriotic things when they believe God is calling them to speak out for peace and justice, righteousness and love for all humankind, including America's political enemies. Freed from the compromising combine of church membership and U.S. citizenship we can now give our primary undivided loyalty to Jesus Christ, who may call us to take positions which may not coincide with those of our own nation.

In our time the most insidious result of the church-nation combine reached it's peak when Hitler took over some of the churches in Nazi Germany to make them tools of his political ambitions. These churches became known as the German Christians. However there were some Christians who stood up to the "emperor." These became known as the Confessing Christians after they drew up the Barmen Declaration. We can affirm with our German brothers and sisters at Barmen in 1933 who declared:

> *Jesus Christ, as he is attested for us in Holy Scriptures is the one Word of God which we have to hear and which we have to trust and obey in life and in death.*
>
> *We reject the false doctrine, as though the Church could and would have to acknowledge as a source of its proclamation, apart from and besides this one Word of God, still other events and powers, figures and truths, as God's revelation.*

But now we see by the statistics that the emperor's reign is ending. . . finally. Constantine took over the Church and clothed himself and his Empire in the Christian religion in order to advance his political purposes. That has changed, and now we can say that "The Emperor has no clothes!" And Christians can follow Jesus only.

–April 3, 2009

NO MORE

In Binghamton, New York at the moment of this writing it is 2:48 PM Eastern Standard Time. In the American Civic Association building forty or so new immigrants have been taking a citizenship exam in preparation for U.S. Citizenship.

While these hopeful applicants for a new life in our country were expressing what U.S. citizenship meant to them, a crazed individual drove up to the back door of the building, parked his vehicle so as to block anyone trying to escape through the rear entrance, went around to the front, entered the building, and began to fire two high powered handguns at innocent staff and students., killing in cold blood thirteen persons, and then killed himself. Four others were wounded and were rushed to local hospitals, before this deplorable act of evil perpetrated by an unknown gunmen was over. By days end the governor will speak, the law enforcement officers will be praised and many will declare that "our" prayers are with the families of those killed.

And in a week's time the media will be working on other stories. Predictably there will be future stories of a similar nature and other families to be prayed for. So goes the endless cycle of gun violence in our own country, the land of the free.

Meanwhile there are unknown participants in this story whose activities will not be covered and who will not face the justice system, because what they have done is considered legal in our society, but whose contribution in this horrific tragedy will have been critically necessary. Without what they did, this despicable episode would not have happened and there would not be grieving families this evening. I point this accusing finger at all those who were involved in the manufacture and distribution of guns, who put the guns of violence in the hands of the murderers, in the Civic Association building in Binghamton today. I also point an accusing finger at the majority of state legislators and members of Congress who, out of fear of the National Rifle Association and assorted gun lovers, have consistently refused to put an end to indiscriminate gun use in this nation.

I am confident that each of these commercial gun makers and dealers as well as each state and federal legislator means no harm to anyone and is innocent of today's murders and those committed everyday. But I believe they are held hostage to an obscenely evil system over which they apparently have little power to thwart.

Until we as a nation rise up with one voice and say NO MORE, the insanely evil system of gun availability and use will continue to shatter innocent lives. It can be done. We did it to the evil system of slavery a hundred and fifty years ago.

–May 17, 2009

I NEED YOU TO BE WRONG

I need you to be wrong so that I can sustain my certainty that I am right. I dare not enter into a dialogue with you lest I begin to doubt my own position. Therefore I must separate myself from you. My sense of rightness requires my departure from your table. I can be in fellowship only with those who are right as I am.

These are the thoughts I imagine to be under the surface in the minds of those who yesterday began the process by which to remove their church from the Presbytery of Yellowstone of the Presbyterian Church U..S.A. I don't know this, because no one from the Springhill Presbyterian Church has told the Presbytery why they want to leave us. At this point my imagination has been stimulated only by rumor and speculation..

Many years ago a prominent Chicago psychiatrist who was a visiting professor in Pastoral Counseling at McCormick Seminary advised us to beware of those who think they have a "private pipeline to God." Am I seeing this prediction and warning coming true in the case of a nearby church? I think so.

I think the deep psychological need of some Christians to be right underlies their conviction of the inerrancy of the Bible, which is the old term for taking the Bible literally–word for word. God is to a great extent beyond our human scrutiny and that makes the one who needs to be right uncomfortable. But the Bible is a different matter. You can hold it in your hand and read every word of it, and if you take the position that every word is from God, then you have the magic key to being right! Whatever conviction you want to flaunt is right–because it's in the Bible.

However, God cannot be "seen" by earth-bound eyes. This is the core truth which the people of the Old Testament knew when they affirmed that whoever looked upon God would die. This is what is meant by the term *holy.* God is holy, separate from us-- in a different realm–beyond space and time and apart from the certainties of men and women. What we know of God is what God has chosen to reveal to us–to the degree that we perceive God's revelation.

Thus, the theology which we develop must be seen as a collection of incomplete approximations, and metaphors. Our thoughts about God and what God wants of us must always be open to correction and expansion, based upon God's continuing revelation to us and our humble and prayerful attempt to gain new insights from God. This developing theology is greatly enhanced by honest dialogue with others who also are seeking to grasp God's revelation to them. Such spiritual growth is stifled by the certainty that one possesses the full truth of God on a particular issue or question.

Conflict in the church and in society grows with the rigid unwillingness to enter into dialogue with those of other theological, ethical or political positions. In the church this reaches its extreme limits when one decides to separate oneself from those who have other positions. An old favorite Bible quote for such brothers and sisters is *Come ye out from among them.* On the other hand, Jesus' willingness to relate to tax collectors and other sinners is really quite the opposite of this separatist position.

Well, that's what I think–but then, I could be wrong, since God has not given me a *private pipeline* as some may feel they possess*!*

–June 2, 2009

NO ROOM IN PARADISE

For the last forty-one years there has been a small meditation chapel along highway 89 between Livingston, Montana and Yellowstone Park. It is located in what is known as Paradise Valley. Over the years visitors from all over the world have registered their appreciation for this serene space along life's way, filling almost 5,000 visitor log pages. It was built by a group of Christian men and women years ago and placed on private land on a slight cliff beside the road. Up until now a succession of owners of the land have gladly permitted the chapel. But the new owners of the ground under the chapel want it removed by July first. Because the new owners "have plans that do not include the chapel." (Bozeman Daily Chronicle, June 23, 2009)

No room in paradise for the chapel, at least not in their back yard. This is difficult to comprehend since the location is on the edge of a cliff where no farm machinery is going to dare to be, and since the tiny 10' by 14' chapel barely uses 200 square feet of the new owners' property.

In a larger sense these unknown new owners reflect unwittingly the mood and value judgment of contemporary culture. This contemporary viewpoint might be characterized by such thoughts as these:"We've made our plans for Sunday, and they don't include church. In fact I've set out on my life plan, which precludes any input from anyone else, including–especially-- God."

So as this little chapel is removed from the busy roadside, somehow it is indicative of the removal of God from our busy lives. We are intent upon creating our own paradise in which there is no room for the chapel. My wife and I went to a church college which provided daily chapel services as well as other religious events. Now, as we prepare to attend the 60th reunion of our class, we note in the latest report of the Board of Trustees of our college that there is no mention of its Christian life or heritage. Those four years spent in college for Doris and me were indeed paradise. Now there is no room for chapel in paradise.

I have been reminded lately of a very interesting village-type museum in Hardin, Montana. Among the buildings which have been brought in to create this nostalgic view of the past is a small church building, formerly a German Evangelical Church from that area of the state. When one enters the little sanctuary, it seems sterile, unused, and sad. It is merely a musty empty old building, devoid of life–human or divine. Perhaps the best that can be said as one leaves to view other museum buildings is *How quaint!*

Perhaps the little chapel from Paradise Valley will find its way into some museum somewhere to show our children how quaint things used to be.

WRY BREAD... food for thought with a wry twist
–October 3, 2009

"ALL WE LIKE SHEEP:"

An Associated Press news story in this morning's paper reports on a recent Pew Research Center poll, which shows that there are decreasing numbers of people in the U.S. who believe that the world is getting warmer–only 57%. In April of last year many more, 71%, thought we are getting warmer. Among those who admit that the world is getting warmer, only a third think we are to blame, down from almost one half who a year ago believed human activity such as carbon emissions to be the culprit.

While the public's belief in global warming is decreasing sharply, the scientific community is in increasing agreement about global warming and humankind's influence in this serious problem. What is going on here to make our concern for the environment diminish while scientists are ever more concerned about global warming and the future of the planet? Either the general public is not listening to the voices of science and reason, or we have found other "authorities" whom we allow to shape our opinions. Powerful voices, such as the haranguing of conservative talk radio hosts, on a daily basis are ridiculing the grim forecasts of those who would warn us of environmental deterioration.

I wish I had the ability to draw a cartoon to express what I am feeling about this matter. In place of pencil and paper, let me try to fill in your imagination of such a cartoon!

Picture a rather large open lifeboat filled with people seated in the boat on church pews. They are facing a pulpit in the bow with a man in clerical collar and garb preaching to the survivors in the boat. His face is easily recognizable as one of the more well known talk show hosts. In the cartoon bubble over his heard are his words to the crowd: ***"I assure you, folks, we are NOT sinking, as some would have you believe!"*** A closer look at the boat shows that it is indeed going down, taking on water, listing at an unsteady angle and the water has reached up to the pew benches and rising. Look now at the faces of the doomed congregation. Can you detect the appearance of sheep?

"All we like sheep have gone astray. . . ."

–November 27, 2009

"ME-ISM REVISITED AND REVISED"

In a front page article in the Bozeman Daily Chronicle on November 27, 2009, under the headline: "High price of health care worries Americans," a woman in Ackworth, Georgia is quoted as proclaiming:

"Well, for one, I know nobody wants to pay taxes for anybody else to go to the doctor–I don't want to pay for somebody to use my money that I could be using for myself."

For me this woman's confession of values stands out as a remarkably clear example of what Robert Bellah and associates labeled as *Me-ism* in Habits of the Heart. This book was the result of extensive sociological research conducted in the 1960s to study attitudes of commitment to community. Individualism emerged as a dominant attitude among contemporary Americans. Bellah cited such a belief system called Sheila-sm which a woman named afer her own name.

Is it any wonder that health care for all Americans may very well be a hollow dream? Sheila-sm puts in jeopardy all attempts to provide anything beyond Emergency Room treatment (if that) for our impoverished neighbors. And, yes, they are our neighbors. Whether they live on our street or "across the tracks," whether they are in plain sight or invisible, or whether they resemble us or not, they are our neighbors.

But the more critical question is "Am I their neighbor?" There is a switch-frequently unnoticed-- in the story of the Good Samaritan in

Luke. While the rich man asked Jesus to identify who might be his neighbor, Jesus challenged the rich man to be a neighbor by showing what a true neighbor does. In effect he said that a neighbor extends health care to the person beside the road. In the issue at hand, the neighbor willingly pays taxes so that people who have no health insurance or care may go to the doctor.

Jesus challenged the "well heeled" to "hoof" it over to the side of the road where people are hurting and there to be a neighbor to those in need; not to recite the slogan of those who pass by on the other side of the road: *I don't want to pay for somebody to use my money that I could be using for myself."*

But turn to another page in today's Chronicle and let Jesus ask "Which do you think is a neighbor to those beside the road?" In the words of the Chronicle editorial, true neighbors are "the students (who) had raised $7000 to donate to the Central Asia Institute to help with its school building efforts," as their response to Bozeman's Greg Mortenson's work of building schools in impoverished villages in Pakistan and Afghanistan over the past few years. The school children said in effect, *We want to use some our money to help build schools for children elsewhere in the world who do not have schools.* That is anything but me-ism.

–December 11, 2009

(God) in PARENTHESES?

I am indignant. I take umbrage at a guest editorial I read in today's "Bozeman Daily Chronicle" on the opinion page in which the author appears to "write off God" and put God in a parenthesis. A retired English professor at Montana State University uses the story of "The Emperor's New Clothes" to point out many Americans' denial of certain political and economic truths facing us today. Instead of seeing the naked truth of poverty, joblessness, and all the rest of the fall-out of the economic crisis, the author observes that we traffic in "half truths and outright lies" to keep us from facing the naked truth, pretending instead that our economy is after all clothed, so to speak. So far, so good.

But then the author tries her hand at theology and puts God in a parenthesis. Here is what she writes: "It's actually kind of comforting to live with a naked king who thinks he's gorgeously dressed, if he's your king (or treasured belief or ideology)." I hear the author equating my "treasured belief or ideology" with the half truths and outright lies with which we hide ourselves from the naked truth that the emperor has no clothes–i.e. that our society is steeped in huge injustices and other forms of interpersonal violence–that my Christian faith is a form of self-delusion. Actually this goes along with the all too frequent charge leveled at those of us who believe in God, that such nonsense is used as a comfort by naive believers as they face death or any other bad thing in life. Thus God is relegated to a parenthesis which contains an extraneous or irrelevant idea or interlude added to an otherwise complete sentence. There it is! To an increasing number of people their life is quite complete without God.

And yet, I believe that without God the sentence has been completed for us and all humanity. By our own actions we have been sentenced to the chaos and darkness of unlimited greed and violence.

To resolve the problems in our society, the author suggests that: "The darkness invites us to go inward, to restore energy and relationships. Without compassion and loving kindness, the threads of interconnectedness cannot be woven, and the light cannot be seeded that nurtures the coming of spring." This inward quest, it is implied, might very well be made at Christmas time.

I agree with the need for compassion and loving kindness in order to connect with our neighbors near and far. But I do not believe that the resource for this level of human life and relationship can be found within ourselves.

Now let me try my hand at theology! Christmas, it seems to me, is anything but an inward journey. Rather, it celebrates a holy journey from far outside the human situation–from God– to us, not from within us. Thus it is from God that we are given the gift of compassion and loving kindness. God is not to be relegated to the parenthetical. Instead, God is the central source of our capacity for positive relationships and interconnectedness.

–January 14, 2010

A DISASTER AFTER A DISASTER

While the earthquake in Haiti has brought a disaster of unthinkable devastation and loss of life, what Pat Robertson said on his so-called Christian Network the day after the Haitian disaster was, I think, a disaster of unthinkable proportions which could cause a profound loss of credibility to the Christian Faith. According to a Tribune Washington Bureau news release picked up by the Bozeman Daily Chronicle, *Robertson blamed the earthquake in Haiti on a "pact with the devil" purportedly entered into by the Haitian people in a bid to defeat French colonization in the early nineteenth century.* Apparently Robertson concludes that all the trouble the Haitian people have had since 1791 including this week's 7.9 earthquake, is a result of a curse put upon them by the "devil" who in turn freed them from the French. And Robertson had the audacity to say this to his listeners yesterday.

In my opinion, Pat Roberson has spewed a wad of ancient pre-Christian superstitious rot under the banner of his so-called Christian declaration. In my opinion, to label as Christian what this man has said publicly is an absolute disaster in its own way, which comes upon the heels of the horrific disaster in Haiti two days ago.

The clear implication in the report of Robertson's statement is that, though God did not bring the disastrous earthquake upon the people, it was the devil who brought this curse of devastation down upon the Haitians as the most recent result of the Haitians promise to serve the "devil."

I am deeply troubled by two aspects of Robertson's response to this disaster in Haiti. (1) He seems to say that the earthquake is their fault as a nation, thus showing a grievous lack of compassion for the Haitian victims of this terrible event. (2) Robertson appears to assign to something or someone whom he calls "the devil" divine status and power. That there was a pact with the devil, and that the devil placed a curse upon Haiti, and that the earthquake has been caused by the devil reveals that Robertson believes that there is a divine, albeit evil, power other than God and in addition to God.

As a Christian I believe in the one and only true God who in Jesus Christ expresses his forgiving love for humankind, and that there simply is no other divine power or being. Thus I am deeply offended when anyone claiming to expound a Christian message speaks of two divinities. What a disaster to talk this way.

–April 2010

PIETY ON THE LEFT

A recent issue of "The Week"(April 2, 2010) reports on a study conducted by Canadian psychologists in which "they found that people who purchase environmentally friendly items feel a 'moral glow' that makes them more likely to cheat and act selfishly in their private lives." The key word in this for me *moral glow*. I would characterize *moral glow* as the feeling of self righteousness one is apt to enjoy after having done something difficult but morally good, or from having deprived oneself of something pleasurable and enticing on moral grounds.

Traditionally, self righteousness is a condition we have most always assigned to those on what has come to be called the religious right. *Fundamentalists*, we used to call them. Piety on the right. But in the past few decades it has become apparent that there is also a piety on the left as in the case of those studied in Canada.

Whether you look with superior disdain at an obese person consuming a cheeseburger in a fast food restaurant, or you condemn your neighbors for playing cards; whether you fault your neighbors for failing to recycle aluminum cans or you wag your finger at those who go dancing your self-righteous moral glow is much the same. The "sins" are different but the moral condemnation is the same. And the *moral glow*, I assume is much the same.

So far as the connection between moral glow and moral laxity, which the Canadian psychologists have isolated, The sexual wanderings of Jimmy Swaggert and the financial and sexual exploits of Jim Bakker, who with his wife, Tammy Faye led the *Praise the Lord* television network a few years ago may be examples. It is more difficult to find examples among the less well-known, but it makes you wonder! Maybe that's the explanation for the socially sensitive liberal who tears up his parking tickets out of contempt for the lowly cop.

Beware of piety on the right or the left!

–June 2010

A CITY AND A TOWER WITH ITS TOP IN THE HEAVENS?

A team of scientists have computer designed the DNA for a microrganism. They have fabricated this new DNA. By using a host cell they have brought to life their newly designed organism, calling her *Synthia.* In an obscure laboratory somewhere in the U.S. in the year 2010 a sacred line has been crossed, albeit with the help of a living host cell. A living thing has been created by a group of human beings.

Some point to the enormous potential for good because we will now be able to create new sources of nourishment and energy. Others envision mammoth evil stemming from this break-through, which will enable people with malicious intent to design swarms of lethal organisms bent upon human destruction.

Once again, as with genetic engineering and the cloning of certain species there are those who charge that we are "playing God." One of the survivors of the BP oil rig debacle in the Gulf of Mexico, under which the gigantic oil gush is now occurring, had uttered the caution that we are "messing with 'Mother Nature'." Yes! Apparently that is what we mortals are doing these days. The created ones are not only messing with creation, but we are now *creating*!

It would appear that the final nail has been driven into the coffin into which rationalist "enlightened" humanity has dumped God. One observer says it this way. "The ability to design and create life is no longer the prerogative of the gods."

What are we to think? The common view, as shaped by the Enlightenment and largely unchallenged in our scientific technological age, is that *whatever there is to be discovered should be found, and whatever can be made should be made.* This compulsion is like the serious mountain climber's response to the question: "Why do you climb to the summit?" "IT'S THERE."

The question of whether or not we should figure out how to create life and then go ahead and do it, if the question ever comes up, is typically not seen as a moral or theological issue. However, I believe a Christian is called to think theologically regarding any and all matters which come to his or her attention. And in the light of such theological reflection to act responsibly and faithfully.

We turn to the Bible to find illumination on the subject at hand. The first eleven chapters of the first book of the Bible, Genesis; give us foundational theological building blocks on which to base our perspective and judgments upon life's questions. You cannot read this material literally, lest we be off looking for snakes that talk and splinters from the boat mentioned in the sixth chapter and following. But that doesn't mean one can skip over these important chapters. The message found in these ancient primal myths must be taken very seriously.

The very first chapter of Genesis provides this foundation stone:

Our theological ancestors believed that *the God who made everything out of nothing directs humankind to* ***have dominion over creation for the good of humankind.***

The story of creation in the second chapter of Genesis gives us the mandate for scientific discovery, which I believe can be read as follows: "God brought all that he made to humankind and asked humans to name all that God had made" Thus it is a foundational truth that ***Humankind is to discover all that can be known of all of God's creation.***

The third chapter of Genesis gives us the ancient belief of our ancestors that: ***Humankind must not come to know all that God knows.***

The eleventh chapter of Genesis is the story of the Tower of Babel. On one level this story sets forth the ancient Israelite explanation of why there are so many languages among people world-wide. But there is a more profound foundational truth here.

Our theological ancestors believed that ***huankind must not ascend to God's level of accomplishment.***

Taken together, these foundational stories give us the mandate to discover all that can be known of all of nature, to care for and to use the natural world and all its resources in a responsible way for the good of humankind. In carrying out this mandate we seem to have unlimited capacities for this task, but we must limit ourselves to our role as creatures and we must not live as though we are supplanting God. The result of dethroning God and taking God's place would be catastrophic for us and our neighbors around the globe.

When we first learned how to release nuclear energy and developed the first nuclear weapons of mass destruction were made, and indeed used on innocent Japanese populations, the question of whether we should have unleashed the power of nuclear energy was seriously raised. Currently millions of gallons of crude oil are being leaked daily at the bottom of the Gulf of Mexico and this toxic mess is polluting the gulf and its shorelines, killing wildlife and despoiling the environment catastrophically. I, for one, wonder if we should cease to take oil from the ocean floor–anywhere on earth.

It is not at all simple to arrive at a Christian approach to these modern-day problems which confront humankind. For many Christians the easy answer is sought by reading the Bible literally to find out what the Bible says about the issue at hand. When one is limited to this method of determining God's will regarding our current dangers and catastrophes, one finds that the Bible has nothing to say about nuclear energy and weapons. Oil spills in the ocean are not mentioned and micro-organisms fall "under the radar" in the Bible's view of things. And so also with a whole host of other issues about which Christians ought to be wrestling in our time.

Determining a Christian perspective upon contemporary issues is a much more complex effort. The earnest and thinking Christian must hold the foundational truths and values as we have tried to express them, and then try to gain a sense of the moral and ethical values which pervade the entire Bible. In a sense, this was the search for ultimate value which a Scribe presented to Jesus. Jesus' answer provides us with the summation of the Biblical foundation for dealing with issues in every age–including our own:

> ***Love God with your whole being***
> ***Love your neighbor as yourself***

With regard then to our developing ability to create living micro-organisms from inanimate chemical components, Christian value judgements will at the very least make us extremely wary and cautious, and make us open to self-restraint if we conclude God so directs us.

As God's creatures we are not the masters of the universe. Rather, God has made us stewards of the natural world and directed us to act in such a way as to contribute to the greatest good for the greatest number of others.

A city with its tower in the heavens? We can do it, but shall we? Think about it!

–September 10, 2010

"DELIVER US FROM EVIL"

National Public Radio reported this morning on a small desert village in the Negeb in which the Bedouin residents have suffered the destruction of almost all of their houses and buildings in their village at the hands of Israeli soldiers. Repeatedly. Three times in the past year Israeli tractors have invaded this unarmed town and tore it down. One of the now homeless residents earnestly asked a reporter. "How can people do such a thing as this?" Indeed one must ask this question of the entire Middle East. "How can this bloody violence persist among feuding groups year after year for decades since 1948?"

I believe that the answer to these painful question lies in the earlier decades of the twentieth century when evil of colossal proportion was unleashed in the fatal persecution, torture and mass execution of Jews and others under the crazed Nazi regime. When the Nazi scourge was defeated by the Allied armies and many displaced Jews were re-settled in a new homeland in the Middle East, the persistent evil of internecine violence resurfaced in the continuing Jewish-Palestinian violence during succeeding decades of the twentieth century and into the twenty-first. Evil unleashed stalks the earth still.

In our own country the present inhumane treatment of blacks is the continuing legacy of the horrible evil of slavery. In the Fall of 1854 Abraham Lincoln struggled mightily over how he would express his anti-slavery position in a debate with Stephen A. Douglas in Peoria, Illinois. Among the issues he had to come to grips with was the question of what would happen to almost a half a million slaves if they were freed and disbursed into the American society. He could see that the evil of a slave holding society would resurface in other ways. In his words: "to free them all, and keep them among us as underlings" he surmised would not improve their lot to any great extent. As we well know, his speculation was correct. Once unleashed, evil stalks the earth.

Ancient Israelites put it this way: "I the Lord your God am a jealous God, punishing children for the iniquities of their parents, to the third and fourth generation of those who reject me." (Deuteronomy 5:9)

I believe that only God can remove the huge bloody stain of evil. History shows that we cannot on our own rid the world of evil. But God has revealed that it is his redemptive work to remove evil from the world. We are to pray for the removal of evil and its legacy and to be shown how we are to take part in this redeeming work of the removal of evil. When Jesus taught us to pray: **Deliver us from evil,** I believe he was calling us at the same time to offer our efforts and lives in pursuit of that prayer.

–September 10, 2010

THE MISSION OF THE CHURCH ON THE EDGE OF CULTURE

Oak Park, Illinois was a typical white, middle class/upper middle class suburb of Chicago. It was the town in which I grew up, going to high school at a time when it was widely thought that everybody went to church, mostly to Protestant churches, alyhough some to the Catholic churches, and in very rare exceptions to a Jewish synagogue–in Chicago. This was in the 1940's before World War II. We were experiencing the last decades of the Christian Era–Christendom, which had begun in the fourth century with Emperor Constantine's decree that Christianity was to be the official religion of the empire. The mission of the church in the final centuries of the Christian era was summed up Jesus' words found in Matthew 28:19-20:

> *Go therefore and make disciples of all nations, baptizing them in the name of the Father and of the Son and of the Holy Spirit, and teaching them to obey everything that I have commanded you.*

One of the favorite hymns which our high school youth group loved to sing expressed this world-wide mission emphasis:

> *We've a story to tell to the nations,*
> *That shall turn their hearts to the right. . .*

A story of truth and mercy,
A story of peace and light.

We've a Savior to show to the nations,
Who the path of sorrow hath trod,
That all of the world's great peoples
Might come to the truth of God

For the darkness shall turn to the dawning,
And the dawning to noonday bright,
And Christ's great Kingdom shall come on earth,
The Kingdom of love and light.
---written in 1896 by Colin Sterne

We sang the national Westminster Fellowship hymn lustily at each of our Sunday evening youth group meetings:

Youth at work are binging God's own glory
To the earth from Heaven above!

Parenthetically, I cannot help but comment that, soon after our high school graduation in 1945 many of the boys in our youth group went off to war instead!

By the 1980's and certainly by the turn of the new century, the relationship between the Christian church and the American culture had radically shifted from the center of society to its edge. Christian majority participation and influence had disappeared–sadly to many of us in society. And the missionary movement of the 19th century had somewhat diminished. Western societies had become multi-cultural and religiously pluralistic. Christian moral and ethical values no longer held as the consensus of the general population. Perhaps most obvious has been the decline in church attendance and the explosive growth of other activities to occupy Sunday mornings for huge numbers, young and old, in society today.

Those who were beginning to understand this new relationship between the Christian Faith and our culture, called it the Post Christian

Era, finding that the church had been moved from the center to the edge of society, a place shared by other religious traditions. Faith had become; at best, optional and at worst, totally irrelevant to the important things going on in the culture. Today, those with Christian faith find themselves oftentimes at odds with prevailing attitudes and behavior.

There are many Christian groups who see decline in church attendance and moral laxity as sinful trends in society which must be reversed. A great deal of moral persuasion has been aimed at a hoped for return to "family values." Efforts are being made to put public prayers back into civil life in schools and at other public gatherings. I see the development of mega churches as attempts to bring the entire society "back to church." The so called "Christian Right" is a force in national politics attempting to re-Christianize America, sometimes confusing Christian values with American values of free enterprise and military superiority. School boards around the country have been persuaded to put "creationism" into the curriculum at least on an equal footing with the teaching of evolution. These, I believe, are some of the efforts Christian groups are making to try to bring back the Christian religion to the influential center of our culture, which it once occupied. To use a current over-used term, I think such folk are "in denial."

But the changes which have taken place since the 1950's are largely irreversible, I believe, presenting the Christian church in our time and place with critical challenges. Perhaps the most significant run-off from this deluge of change is confusion over the question of ***what now is the mission of the church on the edge of culture?*** We have not been in a position on the periphery of society among groups of other faith commitments, since the centuries before Constantine.

Theologically astute students of the history of the church in the period of official establishment since Constantine observe that the close ties of church and culture have weakened the faith as it has been compromised as it has accommodated to its "parent" culture. Hence the merging of American values and Christian Values. Sometimes Christians who have opposed the position of the United States when it has been engaged in military combat somewhere in the world have been castigated as "Un-American," as well as sinful unbelievers.

However, we are now in an era like that of the early church under Roman rule, when it costs dearly to oppose the prevailing directives of the culture. In the earliest centuries of the church many who refused to worship the Emperor were often persecuted and sometimes killed because of their strong faith. It is against this background in which the church has become a counter-culture that we must try to discern the mission of the Christian church to which God calls us in 21st Century America.

Fortunately God has raised up perceptive thinkers who are leading us in formulating the answers to this critical question. These are theologians who recognize the facts of history that the Christian Faith cannot return to its position of centrality and dominance. Instead they see our position in a Post Christian world as a challenging opportunity for radical, and sometimes costly obedience, to Christ.

For the last few years I have been especially intrigued by the writings of Stanley Hauerwas, a United Methodist theologian, John Howard Yoder, a Mennonite, and most recently Douglas John Hall, of the United Church of Canada, each of whom has been exploring what the mission of the church ought to be in what has been called the Post Modern age or the Post Christian Era.

For Hauerwas the mission of the church is to be God's faithful community in the world bearing witness to peace, love and hope which comes from God.

> *The church must learn time and time again that its task is not to make the world the kingdom of God, but to be faithful to the kingdom by showing to the world what it means to be a community of peace. Thus we are required to be patient and never lose hope. . . hope in God who has promised that faithfulness to the kingdom will be of use in God's care for the world. . . hope in God's faithful caring for the world.*

John Howard Yoder argued, the primary responsibility of Christians is not to take over society and impose their convictions and values on people who don't share their faith, but to "be the church". By refusing to return evil for evil, by living in peace, sharing goods, and doing deeds of charity as needs and opportunities arise. The church witnesses, says Yoder, to the fact that an alternative to a society based on violence or the threat of violence is possible. Yoder claims that the church thus lives in the conviction that God calls Christians to imitate the way of Christ in his absolute obedience, even if it leads to their deaths, for they, too, will finally be vindicated in resurrection.

Yoder counsels patience as Christians seek to live the way of Christ's absolute obedience to God with the assurance that God's way will be ultimately claimed as right in the resurrection.

> *The key to the obedience of God's people is not their effectiveness but their patience. The triumph of the right is assured not by the might that comes to the aid of the right, which is of course the justification of the use of violence and the other kinds of power in every human conflict; the triumph of the right, although it is assured, is sure because of the power of the resurrection and not because of any calculation of causes and effects, nor because of the inherently greater strength of the good guys. The relationship between the obedience of God's people and the triumph of God's cause is not a relationship of cause and effect but one of cross and resurrection.*

Douglas John Hall identifies promoting justice and love as the task of a disestablished Church in our time, not by dominating culture but through witness and service in what I would describe as acting as a catalyst to bring about justice and love in the world.

Hall sets forth his challenge:

> *What then is the mission of a church that can no longer count on its favored status in Western civilization to ensure its meaning and its continued existence? I believe the very first responsibility of Christian communities in*

such a situation was (a) to begin at last to recognize the radical incompatibility of Christian establishment with the biblical and best traditional conceptions of the Christian movement, and (b) to explore the possibilities of Christian witness and service from a position outside or on the edge of the dominant culture.

Instead of clinging to absurd and outmoded visions of grandeur, which were never Christ's intention for his church, serious Christian communities ought now to relinquish triumphalistic dreams of majority status and influence in high places and ask themselves about the possibilities of witnessing to God's justice; and love from the edges of the empire–which is where prophetic religion has always lived. Instead of mourning their losses or naively hoping for their recovery, Christians who are serious about their faith ought to ask themselves why all the metaphors Jesus uses to depict his "little flock" are metaphors of smallness: salt, yeast, light–small things that can serve larger causes because they do not aim to become big themselves.

As I read these three theologians, taken together, I find that the task of the church is to bear witness to the yeast (the Kingdom of God) which is already within the world, at work lifting humankind toward a more just and loving society. This does not mean merely identifying what God is doing, but to take part in God's redeeming activity as a catalyst helping to bring about change toward justice, peace and love.

It seems to me that the words of the prophet, Micah, sum up the contemporary emphasis of the mission of the church on the edge of culture in this Post-Christian Era:

What does the Lord require of you but to do justice, and to love kindness, and to walk humbly with your God. (Micah 6:8)

While Jesus' command to share the Faith still stands, there is a critical need in our time to work toward justice and to relate to others in love and kindness. Furthermore there is a renewed desire for a deepening spirituality, ("to walk humbly with your God") which in a sense is also a mission emphasis required today.

Thus, we labor as Christ's obedient apostles on the edge of our culture, assured of the inexorable growth of God's kingdom in the world, which Jesus taught is *like a mustard seed, the smallest of seeds, but when it is grown it is the greatest of shrubs-- it becomes a tree, so that the birds of air come and make nests in its branches. (Matthew 13:31-32)*

–August 2011

FROM THE PIT, THE PINNACLE

I am struck with shame and anger when two hugely contrasting news stories appear back to back, as they did today. FEMA (Federal Emergency Management Administration is about out of funds, and they have just begun to care for people in the Eastern seaboard who have lost everything in the wake of hurricane Irene and the devastating rains and flooding which she has brought. Houses have been destroyed, the power is out, and there is a terrifying shortage of food and water.

In the news on the same daily is reported that a NFL player has signed a one hundred million dollar contract with the owners of his team. From the pit of human misery we see the pinnacle of human greed. While we, as a nation, are pouring out billions on the wars we are fighting in the Middle East, funding for dire human need in our country is running out. While some east-coast football fans will have no TV and now living room to watch the NFL this Fall, thousands of their fellow citizens will be paying extravagant prices to watch the multi million dollar contracts to be played out. From the pit, the pinnacle. What has become of us in the "land of the free an home of the brave?"

Another huge tragic story in the news comes to us from Africa. While thousands are starving to death in the horn of Africa, rebel troops in Libya, having toppled their tyrant dictator have walked into his sumptuous palace and uncovered traces of overwhelming personal wealth and evidence of an unbelievably costly life-style. From the pit, the pinnacle.

A similar sharp social inequity is to be seen in the growing disparity in our economy between the six and seven figure incomes of corporate CEOs and other people of wealth in the midst of a growing percentage of Americans requiring food stamps and the shameful frequency of homeless neighbors living on the streets and in the doorways of most of the cities in the U.S Again the pinnacle and the pit.

What is to become of our world? In Libya, as in other such societies, after years of crushing inequities of wealth and power, the poor and the disenfranchised have risen up from the pit and stormed the castle on the pinnacle.

Could such a thing happen here? In this land presumably imbued with "liberty and justice for all?

–September 8, 201

COUNTING FOR SOMETHING, OR JUST COUNTING

In reading a novel by a British mystery writer, whom I enjoy, I came across a quote which I find profound. M.C. Beaton has put a succinct quote at the beginning of each chapter in his story, Death of a Village. The quote for Chapter Seven is:

> *Man is the only animal that laughs and weeps; for he is the only animal that is struck with the difference between what things are, and what they ought to be.*

Written by William Hazlitt, an eighteenth century British philosopher and essayist, this assessment of the nature of a human being adds credibility to the assertion that there is a qualitative difference between man and all other animal species.

It makes good television entertainment when a trainer presents a dog which can count. Two objects are presented and his dog intelligently barks on numerical command twice and so on. The dog can count! We are intrigued by studies which show near human characteristics and activities in primates.

Serious scholarship has also tried to show the continuity between "lower" species and the human species, often seeming to imply that the differences are only ones of degree, that the traits we possess are merely more highly developed forms of traits our animal ancestors possess. I think of Carl Sagan as one of the well known scientists who put forth this limited view of human nature. To be sure, I believe there is an evolutionary development among the species including the human creature A dog can count and we can do mathematics, just a higher form of counting. But, I also believe there is a significant discontinuity between us and the others on the evolutionary chart.

William Hazlitt says, we can laugh and weep! And that is because we perceive the difference between what is and what ought to be, a distinction which animals cannot make.. We weep when a promising young person is killed in a car crash. That young person *ought* to have had many more years to come. My cat did not weep when he killed a young mother bird, leaving starving babies in the nest.

We laugh at incongruity. I like to pun. The humor in a pun comes from a mix-up of words making words mean what they really *ought not* to mean. Like the customer with her dog on a leash in a nursery looking at a currant bush. She asks the nurseryman the charge, and he says, "The charge for this current bush is 120 volts." She laughs, but her dog does not.

Our ability to tell the difference between what we are and what we ought to be is the basis of our moral consciousness. I think this moral perception is one very important trait in our humanity giving us the basis for making a difference in our world. You might say that with this ability we can count for something in our lifetime–rather than just counting, as some trained dogs can do.

WE OUGHT TO BRING BACK "OUGHT!"

William Hazlitt wrote that we humans have the capacity to distinguish between "IS" and "OUGHT," and that lower animals are unable to distinguish between what is and what ought to be. Born in the 18th century and living into the 19th century, Hazlitt wrote during a time and in a culture in which *ought* was an operative word for a commonly agreed upon impulse. It seems to me that in his time there was a pretty clear consensus about how one should live–not that everyone attained such a level of behavior, but at least most folks knew what *ought* to be–how one ought to live, what kind of a world ours should be.

I am not so sure this can be said of us today, for we live in a time when all authority is questioned. The current rejoinder to a declaration of what ought to be is likely to be "Who said so?" It is commonly held that what ought to be is anyone's call. It seems to me that these days many feel that morality is in the mind of the doer, just as beauty is in the eye of the beholder. Neither beauty nor good is considered absolute. It is whatever you say is good–or wrong. Thus, I think, the substantive meaning of the word, OUGHT, has been significantly diminished and distorted, if not totally removed.

By implication then, if we take Hazlitt seriously, we seem to have lost something of our humanity! And so, I think, we ought to bring back OUGHT!

WORDS TO THE WISE?

Recently CNN presented a follow-up on the Jonestown Massacre through interviews with survivors. One woman who had gone through this horrible experience, but survived, when asked about her religious faith at this point in her life, answered. "I'm not religious but I am spiritual." She went on the say that she has no use for organized religion. This anti-religious claim to be spiritual is heard with increasing frequency these days.

Two acclaimed writers have written under the same title: *THE FUTURE OF FAITH.* In 1999 John Updike in an article in "The New Yorker" commented upon declining church membership and attendance had this to say. "Home study and the Sunday-morning religious shows on television are cutting into church attendance. As part of the do-it-yourself trend, the sales of religious books have risen spectacularly, by fifty percent in the last ten years."

Harvey Fox, retired professor of divinity at Harvard, writes in a book just published, "increasing numbers of .people who might once have described themselves as 'religious,' but who want to distance themselves from the institutional or doctrinal demarcations of conventional religions now refer to themselves as "spiritual." but not religious.

Of the many in our time who have departed from the church, some angrily and others passively, apparently a significant number still seek contact with God, or at least with things of the spirit. And yet contact with God and things of the spirit are what the churches have historically offered. Like a thirsty person declining the offer of a glass of water, what organized religion purports to offer is being rejected.. What is going on here?

When the Jonestown survivor vehemently declared that she rejects organized religion she spoke for many survivors of an oppressive religious past in their lives. Jonestown was oppression to the absolute extreme. But could it be that there are elements of oppression to be found in traditional church life which we have experienced.? And which could cause people to forsake the church?

Jim Jones so dominated the thinking and wills of the members of his cult that they were robbed of their freedom and their lives were crushed. When any religious institution dominates the thought and wills of its adherents, there will be those who react by rejecting their connection with that religious institution, or any other form of organized religion.

Such institutional domination may take the form of imperatives directed at members by the hierarchy under which the local congregation is obligated, or by particular declarations and/or exhortations of the local clergy. This domination often is the imposition of detailed creedal statements or moral standards as a qualification for membership. In many cases or a culture of self-righteous piety may subtly dominate the lives of the members of the religious group.

Much of this domination results in an atmosphere of exclusivity in which those who do not hold the group's views or conduct themselves in approved ways are left outside the group and are considered wrong and unworthy. In this atmosphere no questions can be asked nor can divergent opinions be expressed.

When a religious institution restricts freedom of thought and action there are many who will choose to reject membership in that group and its dominating claims. This negative reaction to the dominating by religious groups and; their leaders accounts for a significant loss of membership and activity in such churches today.

But what of those who have left behind religious affiliation which has not been oppressive and restricting? Mainline churches with a democratic and interactive approach to the education of their membership are experiencing troubling declines in membership. Reasons for this loss are more difficult to explain. Indeed, I think, there are many different reasons for dropping church from the lives of people in our culture today.

To a growing number, Sunday worship and whatever else their church offers seem dull and un-engaging compared to the multiplicity of entertainment and/or media delights available 24/7. In pondering this question, John Updike writes. "Perhaps the future of faith lies all about us, in the proliferating escapism and induced hysteria of 'entertainment,' with the intimidating, mind-blowing enlargement that electronic media have made possible. We are surrounded by entertainment more completely than medieval man was by the church and its propaganda. Feeling despondent and lonely? Turn on the television set." (The New Yorker, November 29, 1999, p.90).

Others have rejected the Christian faith on rational intellectual grounds. During this year's Christmas season a national association of atheists has put up a large billboard in an eastern city (Boston, I think) denouncing the Christmas story as a myth not to be believed or celebrated.

What this exposes, I think, is the flattening of religion into a set of strictly rational propositions, which modern science contests.

When Christian Faith is limited to a set of beliefs requiring ascent, and when churches are seen to offer nothing beyond propositions to be believed there are those who turn from the churches looking for something more. This appears to account for increasing numbers of charismatic churches, and a rising interest in Eastern Religions, and New Age Religion which offer a more mystical experience than do traditional Christian religions.

I think that there are Christians who are impatient with their church's tepid approach to society's ills. They are strongly motivated toward action on social, justice issues and when they find little happening in their church in this realm they are out the door and heading for the local food bonk to volunteer their time or to join some other action going on in the streets so to speak. I know of campus ministers who no longer can interest students in study groups or worship experiences, but who can successfully enlist students for volunteer efforts designed to help the needy and oppressed in the community

Finally, there are older people who have had long and warm associations with church life, but who today find the worship and other church programs so different that they no longer feel that it is "their church." Some who feel this way leave and look for another church, but others just stay home disappointed that the old familiar comfort is now not available to them. This reaction is especially frequent in turbulent times when so much all around one is in upheaval.

So, does all this point to the demise of the churches? Not if the serious reasons people leave the churches are seen as "words to the wise,". which point to deficiencies in the relevance and faithfulness of churches in this time and place. Words which encourage churches move creatively to address contemporary needs.

–October 2011

FAVORED–YES. . . FAVORITE–NO

Regime change and nation building have played a significant part in the U.S. effort to combat international terrorism, particularly as violent acts have been directed against American interests at home and abroad. This radical intervention into the affairs of other nations by the U.S. is seen by many observers as an imperial foreign policy and as an expression of the concept of American exceptionalism.

This particular sense of national identity has inspired us from as far back as Colonial days. It is the idea that somehow we are quite special among nations and thereby destined to be a model for other nations to follow–"A shining city on a hill." In religious terms we see our nation as favored by God and as God's favorite.

I don't think any discussion of American exeptionalism is complete without referring to the religious origins of this national self affirmation. Historical and sociological analysts of this concept in our history from the beginning point to the earliest emigrants to this continent who saw the similarity of their journey to the new world to that of the Israelites escaping Egyptian captivity and traversing the wilderness in search of the new land God had promised would be theirs. The early settlers are seen to have appropriated God's promise to Israel as God's special blessing upon the nation they were building here on this new continent. God's intended destiny for the Israelites was taken to heart by our own American forebears. *I will be your God, you will be my people and I will give you this land and make of you a great nation. Thus you shall be a light to the nations.*

And now, four hundred years later, there are many who hold to this grand promise and gladly support U.S. foreign policy which reflects this notion that we are not only favored by God, but that we are indeed God's favorite people.

Without a doubt we have been favored in many ways: with an abundance of natural resources, a well developed democratic system and a free society without caste or class. Favored–Yes. But God's favorite nation?

As a Christian I do not believe that God plays favorites among the nations of the earth. We are not God's favorite, nor is any other nation, including Israel. This conviction is expressed in one of the confessions of faith of my particular faith tradition as follows:

"Although nations may serve God's purposes in history, the church which identifies the sovereignty of any one nation or any one way of life with the cause of God denies the Lordship of Christ and betrays its calling."

Thus, to elevate America, its political or economic system as God's favorite is, I believe, idiolatry.

Favored–Yes.. . Favorite–No.

–December 2011

"LOVE AND MARRIAGE GO TOGETHER . . . like a horse and carriage"

It was in 1955–56 years ago–that *"Love and Marriage Go Together Like a Horse and Carriage,"* with lyrics by Sammy Cahn, was introduced by Frank Sinatra in the television production of Thornton Wilder's *Our Town*. It immediately became a hit record. A decade later the truth which this song celebrated began to erode, making way for the changed social panorama of twenty-first century America and other Western countries.

Recently the media was been reporting the latest findings concerning marriage. According to studies recently conducted nearly 50% of American adults are not married. Those who are deciding to marry these days are most often older that their counterparts in the 1950s. Similar findings are coming out of Europe and other Western nations as well. Some observers are saying that the future of marriage as an institution in Western Society is in jeopardy.

In place of marriage there is an increasing prevalence and growing acceptance of couples living together without marriage, and for only as long a period of time as the couple wants to stay together. Where there was once an eagerness on the part of youth in their teens and twenties to marry there is now a reluctance to marry as early in life as was the custom in the past.

A number of developments in the second half of the twentieth century have come together, I believe, which have brought about what can be considered a seismic shift in the social landscape of our society. Not the least of which is the development of convenient birt control methods.

Thornton Wilder wrote *Our Town* in 1938. Its' setting was a typical small town in New England, in which time-honored traditional social and moral values prevailed which were largely unquestioned by audiences watching the play.

A few years later, in 1955, the song, *Love and Marriage Go Together Like a Horse and Carriage,* appeared in the television version of *Our Town.* At that time the traditional social and moral values of Grover's Corner, New Hampshire in *Our Town* were still held by consensus in Western culture, even though an erosion of those values had begun to occur.

Then came significant and far reaching change- producing developments. In 1960 the U.S. Federal Food and Drug Administration approved the use of oral contraceptive pills, which substantially reduced the fear of pregnancy. The availability of mechanical birth control devices had already begun to free men and women in this regard. In 1963 Betty Friedan wrote *The Feminine Mystique* in which she questioned the adequacy of the traditional role of housewife and mother for middle class women in our society.

The need for women to take over traditional male roles during World War II paved the way for the opening up of many new roles for women. The term *Rosie the Riveter* from the 1942 song of the same name became the buzz word for women working at jobs formerly considered only for men. In the early 1900's the women's suffrage movement had broken the trail for *Rosie* and her feminine colleagues in the workforce.

Less easy to pin-point, growing rejection of authority under lay much of what was happening in the second half of the twentieth century. But, as with the sexual revolution and the feminist movement the 1960s have become the time of origin for massive questioning of authority. Many began questioning the rules for personal behavior which had been grounded in tradition based religious teaching. Behavioral decisions were now made by many on the basis of one's own desires and aspirations, rather than on what one's church decreed. Having broken from tradition these self-oriented members of society tended to become models for the behavior of their less innovative followers. Similarly the traditional values of societal, family and group behavior gave way to self-styled values and behavior.

The upshot of all this is that people can now live together as long as they want to, without the commitment of marriage with or without children. Each will have fully satisfying careers in whatever field of endeavor he or she chooses. And there will be no person or institution which will prohibit them from doing as they please.

In ths social shift, as with the explosive technological revolution of our time, the old implements and methods become obsolete as new devices and arrangements take their. place.

So with both the horse and carriage and with marriage as well!

But does this bode well for society as a whole and for the future of our culture? I think not. That is, unless some new rules emerge. I am aware this sounds politically incorrect.

The future depends upon what tangent we are headed. At present it looks like we are moving toward anarchy–everyone for him or herself.

In the world over and from the beginning of human history, societies have always needed and developed some form of social structuring to organize and regulate the relationships of men and women and the propagation and nurture of children. More often than not, it seems to me, religion has been closely tied to the development of such social arrangements in most cultures. As we have seen, such structures in our society are being razed. If approved customs for sexual relationships and the propagation and nurture of children do not develop, the resulting chaos of individual freedom will threaten the future of our culture, I believe.

The more desirable trajectory for us to be on, is the one on which new agreed-upon customs for the ordering of society are forming. It has been observed that when the consensus supporting approved behavior breaks down, oftentimes law takes the place of agreed-upon custom. An example of this is the current debate in state and federal legislatures over the definition of marriage, and whether the word, *marriage* is broad enough to include homosexual couples. The question remains, however, as to whether the passing of laws will result in commonly held customary behavior and the reordering of society.

The more significant question for me has to do with what part can and must religion in our society play in the development of new rules and patterns for sexual activity and child nurturing. There are four interrelated factors, it seems to me, which mitigate against the clear and effective influence of religion upon the development of commonly held behavioral standards.

(1) The growing multiplicity of various religious faiths in our culture today with differing directives for personal and social behavior.
(2) The sharp disagreements within the Christian churches on these issues.
(3) The separation of church and state which has led to the view point commonly held that one's religious faith ought to be separate from secular and political aspects of ones life.
(4) The waning authority of religious principles over individual behavioral choices.

How we overcome these obstacles will greatly affect how our religious commitments in today' society will be able to help to shape the approved standards by which our society functions in the traditional areas of "love" and "marriage."

Therefore, I believe, it behooves all those who have commitment to God in any of the religious faith traditions present in our society to take up the task of helping to re-equip our culture with a viable moral basis for social relationships.

–July 2012

COLLEGIATE MINISTRIES IN 2012

Recently the General Assembly of the Presbyterian Church USA adopted a Vision Statement meant to guide the denomination and its congregations near colleges and universities across the country in a needed renewal and reestablishment of ministry in higher education.

The vision statement is: ***We are a church that reaches, loves and teaches college students to become life-long followers of Jesus Christ.*** While this statement is indeed "simple" and has "elements of evangelism, compassion and education–all hallmarks of reformed ministry." as it is described in an introductory paragraph, its vision, I believe, is nearsighted.

Our vision of faithful ministry in higher education ought to be more farsighted. Our ministry ought to reach into the midst of the academic endeavor of the university itself. I believe the task of the church in higher education is to offer the Christian world view to the academic mix of a multiplicity of ideas and value judgements in a meaningful and intellectually respectable manner, recognizing that ours is but one among many viable world views to be considered as the university seeks to research and teach a full range of ideas and knowledge.

This is not to say that the Christian world view is always missing or inadequately articulated in colleges and universities, but in our society the fear of church-state issues has often prevented an accurate hearing of the Christian point of view. Therefore, it seems to me, that we have the responsibility of offering to fill that gap in some instances, if not many, where the Christian Faith lacks clear expression.

During the years in which I served as a campus minister under the United Ministries in Higher Education the phrase used for this effort was "Helping the university to be itself." That was to say that our task was to assist the university to attain its fullest intended purpose and function. The Christian presence and world view was necessarily, in our view, an authentic aspect of such fullness.

This too, is a hallmark of reformed ministry in higher education.

–September 2012

THE INCARNATION IS IN THE NEWS

There have been many attempts to understand rationally the incarnation of Jesus Christ as affirmed in one way or another by Christians from the very beginning of the Christian Faith. Simply put, the belief in the incarnation is the belief that Jesus was both fully human and fully divine, as irrational and mysterious as that may be.

Recently the news media has reopened this discussion by reporting somewhat sensationally the discovery of what some think is solid evidence that Jesus had been married. This news is taken by some to be a challenge to the Christian belief that Jesus was divine. If this new shred of evidence is authentic it only helps to support the Christian belief that Jesus was fully human, which some over the centuries have doubted. But it has nothing to do with the Christian belief that Jesus was divine.

Any conjecture or evidence that the apostle Paul was married, I suspect would not be as newsworthy as the current news report concerning Jesus' possible marriage. Why? Because Christians do not claim divinity for Paul.

The doctrine of the incarnation of Jesus remains a mystery which continues to be held by Christians.

PART 2

MUSINGS

Here are thoughts of a personal nature: musings about life, occasional journal entries, random memories, and some of my own feelings about life, which I have combined under the tile: MUSINGS.

–January 2006

WHERE WAS I?

Martin Luther King, Jr. Day–some forty years after those days for which he is remembered. The overwhelming feeling I have is summed up in the self-challenge: *Where was I?* The Rev. Ed King, a white Methodist from Mississippi who was engaged in the civil rights movement along with Martin Luther King, Jr. and others, preached in church yesterday and spoke at a breakfast at the Christus Collegium this morning. After the service yesterday a Chronicle reporter asked me what I thought. All I could think to say was that it made me feel guilty for having been so far away and uninvolved. Then I found myself telling about John Worcester's going to Selma on a voter registration mission from seminary in California and that he came from Anaconda and had served as an associate pastor in Bozeman. As if he had been my stand-in. Like those rich young men of privilege who paid for someone else to fight in their place in the Civil War. *Where was I?*

For the generation during my childhood and youth the similar question was *Where were we* during the holocaust? Many Americans fought in the war to topple Hitler, but almost no one in my family. *Where was I?* A month or so too young and in college. Is that answer enough?

These are frustrating and guilt producing questions. Questions for which there is no longer any chance to re-answer. But, what about the issues of today? *Where am I?* Issues like terrible starvation in Africa, freezing homeless people in the mountains of Pakistan, innocent civilian victims of military violence in Iraq, and elsewhere. . . and on and on.

IT'S LONELY IN HERE

Well, it looks like Moscow, Idaho will have a new billboard on Main Street. I must confess to a bit of anger about this. Our daughter, Rose, sent us a clipping from *The Lewiston Tribune* with a front page article headlined: "Moscow billboard will offer humanist message." The message: is: "Don't believe in God? You are not alone."

Karen Frantz, of the American Humanist Association is quoted in the article. "Our purpose was to speak to our population. Unfortunately to speak to our population, we had to speak to everyone." And so a big billboard is to go up on Main Street.

I haven't got this all thought out yet, but here's a start. It seems to me that the reason Karen can't reach other unbelievers without a buck shot approach to the whole population is that by its very nature, unbelief is to be isolated, for it is an essentially self absorbed position. To believe in God or anything else outside oneself is to commit to something outside, worthy of one's devotion. That focal point of one's life tends to bring together others with the same focal point. When one does not believe in anything outside oneself-- some sort of god-- all there is left, is yourself. You become your own focal point. And that is essentially a lonely position to be in.

The billboard message attempts to speak to such loneliness by covering the whole population in order to find the lonely isolated person whose god is his or her own self.

What is offered as an antidote to such loneliness? I'm not sure. I guess I could go to the website listed on the billboard, but I'm not sure I want to.

BELONGING?

As I look back, belonging has been a personal struggle from the beginning. Has it ever been my wold? I wonder? What do I mean by *belonging*? It is to be accepted as a full fledged member of the group–not an outsider–not different . To belong is to be like everyone else especially in terms of values, behavior and interests. And so my not having certain interests, behavior patterns and values which conform to those of others, intensifies my feelings of not belonging.

–2009

WILLIS WAYDE REVISTED

I have re-read John P. Marquand's novel published in 1954, Sincerely, Willis Wayde. I first read it with great appreciation fifty or so years ago. Now in my eighties my feeling about Willis Wayde and his life and times is very different from what it was when I read it as a young man.

In this story Marquand tells of the life of Willis Wayde, who moved to New England with his father and Mother from Colorado in the 1920's when he was a young boy. His father has been hired by a family owned factory near Boston. The Waydes move into a house on the grounds of the mansion in which the owner and his family live–the Harcourts. Young Willis is in awe of the Harcourt's upper class life style and attitudes. As he grows in his association with the Harcourt family and the family enterprise Willis is overwhelmed by the many class differences from his more common upbringing which he experiences in his relationship with the Harcourts and their children and grandchildren especially with Bess, who is Willis's age. Willis struggles to act as the Harcourts and the other upper class New Englanders he meets–a struggle in which, in my earlier reading, Wayde seemed to win his place among the upper class both in business career and in his personal life–much to his delight and mine–at the time.

In the story Willis is given the chance to begin his career in the Harcourt Mill as a sort of apprentice, which leads over time to Willis' ascent in the business world to the point of being able to take over the management and the destiny of the Harcourt Mill. Along with this "rags to riches" climb, Willis Wayde; learns to mimic the life style of the

New England upper class. Unbelievable success comes to him both in business as well as in his personal and family life by the end of the novel.

On one level Sincerely, Willis Wayde is a typical realization of the "American Dream." A dream which I, as a young person shared. I see now why I liked the story. I "was" Willis Wade, and I reveled in his success. I too had grown up among people much higher on the social and economic ladder. Oak Park, my home town was like that. This was impressed upon me in high school after my family moved to a rented flat south of Lake Street. The "real" Oak Park was north of the train tracks and Lake Street. This was the area of large stately houses with deep front lawns stretching to graceful tree line streets. The two flat which we rented was on Oak Park Avenue, a few feet from the curb along which the city busses ran. In those days my favorite family rides were often to the suburbs further out where the rich lived in huge mansions, towns like St. Charles, Batavia and Lake Forest. Lake Forest in which I discovered Willis Wayde built a house later in his career. *Ah yes, if I can only become a Willis Wayde,* I think must have thought as I read the novel fifty or so years ago.

Now, seventeen years after my retirement and around fifty years after my first reading of Marquand's novel, my feeling for Willis Wayde is very different from what it had been. I see now what I believe Marquand wanted his readers to see: that Willis Wayde sold his integrity for success in his career as well as what he thought was his entry into the upper class of New England society. Success enabled him to buy his way into the upper class life style through building himself a mansion like that of the Harcourts.and obtaining all the rest of the accouterments of the upper class in his clothing, how he and his wife furnished their home, his chauffeur-driven Cadillac, and his social relationships.

Intentionally modeling his life after denizens of industry and business, beginning with Mr. Harcourt, Wayde taught himself in a very calculating way to do things as they did, thus overriding his own values, feelings and loyalties

Eventually there came a time when for business reasons Willis Wayde participated in the closing of the Harcourt Mill, an act of disloyalty which he had promised the Harcourt family he would never do. At this point Bess Harcourt, with whom Willis had had a childhood friendship, turns on Willis calling him a *Uriah Heep*, who in Dickens novel, David Copperfield, was condemned for his false humility, insincerity, fraud and treachery.

For all his seeming success, Willis Wayde could not avert Bess's telling blow to his self esteem. She had seen through his insincerity and called him on it. Thus there is a shade of cynicism in Marquand's title of the story of Willis Wayde: Sincerely, Willis Wayde!

Enamored by Wayde's stunning rise, both in business and socially, I did not in my earlier reading understand John Marquand's message. On my second reading, just recently, I have come to see the insincerity of Willis Wayde–and of what would have been my own attempt to attain business and social prominence, had I gone that route.

And so I see that, while I once dreamed of living "the upper class life"(whatever that meant), I did not, however set my course upon such an upward climb. I am now perfectly happy just to be myself—*Sincerely*, Paul Krebill

–2009

THE FOX AND THE HYMN-WRITERS

The day before yesterday in the meeting of the Presbytery of Yellowstone, the Presbyterian Church of Springhill severed its relationship to the Presbytery of Yellowstone and the Presbyterian Church U.S.A. The Presbytery voted 39 to 10 to let this congregation be taken from us. Though the breech was glossed over with a certain amount of nice talk and with the tireless efforts of the Pastoral Team, the pain of defeat and loss on the part of the Presbytery was evident. Within minutes after the vote was counted and reported the delegation from Springhill left the meeting, with what I suspect was a sense of victory and relief.

I had assumed that by this morning I would be able to put all this behind me, but I found myself brooding over what has happened over the past few years in the Springhill Presbyterian Church. An old farm slogan came to me this morning as an accurate metaphor for this situation.

The fox has gotten into the chicken house.

Quite literally, I believe. Some years ago and also recently we left the door ajar and we let into the ministry of the Springhill church pastoral leaders who would ultimately steal the congregation from the membership of this presbytery–as foxes do with chickens when given the opportunity of an open gate

These were the thoughts rumbling through my mind as I went to Sunday worship this morning.

The first hymn jolted me with these words:

But we are vain and sadly proud,
We sow not peace but strife,
Our discord spreads a deadly cloud
That threatens all of life.
–H. Kenn Carmichael
(The Presbyterian Hymnal-- No. 434)

The second song had us singing these words:

Make us one, Lord, make us one;
Holy Spirit, make us one.
Let your love flow so the world will

Know we are one in you.
–Carol Cymbala

The hymn-writers knew about the fox!

–2009

GRAVITY

On the Sunday before Thanksgiving the minister (my son, Dan) asked the children in the children's time what they were thankful for. One little boy said "GRAVITY." At the time I agreed.

Well, at age 82 I'm not so sure. For one thing I'm always dropping things. I haven't been able to figure out why I drop things now more frequently that twenty years ago. But I do know that it is a lot more difficult at my age to bend over to pick stuff up. In those moments I am not all that thankful for gravity. When I climb up the stairs I am not as thankful for gravity as that child is. I don't have the muscle strength of that little kid, so climbing the steps is more difficult now–and I must admit the extra pounds make a difference too.

Another thing is balance. When I asked my doctor about having more problems with balance, He told me that the part of the brain which keeps you steady begins to diminish as one gets older. The Cerebellum, I think it is. Without gravity, balance wouldn't be such a problem. Now I understand why some older people sometimes need canes.

–January 3, 2010

WHERE ONCE MY HYMNS WERE SUNG

The Sunday morning Chronicler announced this morning that today at eleven in the morning Bozeman's "Backburner" jazz ensemble will be playing in the Sola Café on Kagy and Third-- free to any and all who may want to come in for coffee or brunch during that hour. That's the very time which has often been called the "scared hour" of the week when worship is conducted at most Christian Churches across America and in Bozeman as well.

As a regular church-going Christian raised in the first half of the 20th century I can't help but feel offended by this intrusion upon my sacred hour, a competing delight which may very well entice some folk from Sunday morning hymn-singing to jazz at a local up-scale café.

There is irony here, for the Sola is located in a neighborhood commercial strip recently built upon the very site of a Lutheran church which formerly occupied this corner, until it was sold and razed. Where once the hymns were sung the sound of jazz amid the tinkle of coffee cups is now to be heard.

I know (in my head) that things are different now–religious pluralism and cultural diversity and all that, but my values were formed in an earlier time, a time when shops were closed and hymns were sung at eleven o'clock on Sunday morning. Raised in the 1930's my behavior and my emotions were forged on the Constantinian anvil put in place in the fourth century when Emperor Constantine declared he

Christian Religion to be the official religion of the empire. In my heart Constantine still rules.

That's why I can't help but be offended by the Backburner ensemble playing at a time when once my favorite hymns were sung–and when the Christian church is relegated to the backburner!

–2010

TRUE TO LIFE AND APPEALING

For almost twenty years now I have been regularly reading novels. I like to have a "novel going" all the time, so that when I finish one, I can immediately turn to another to begin a new story. Chain reading I guess you'd say.

However I find it quite difficult to find novels which appeal to me. I like novels which are termed "General Fiction" as opposed to Mystery, or Science Fiction, or Intrigue or Thriller or other specialty novels. My own criterion for a good novel is that it be *True to Life*.. To qualify under that standard one would answer "yes" to these questions: (1) Do the characters in this story act and respond as real people would? (2) Is the setting authentic ie. true to the time period and location of the story? (3) Are the events and circumstances reasonable and would things happen as depicted in the story? Furthermore for me to want to read a good *true to life* novel, its period, and location must be what appeal to me, and its people must be one's with whom I would like to spend time. Not all of this is easy to forecast by reading the book summary on the jacket.

I set these standards for the fiction which I write

Having said this I think I ought to be willing to expand my definitions of appealing periods places and people. Expand my comfort zone, so to speak.

–2010

WHAT IS THIS WORLD COMING TO?

Social Change comes hard to many people, especially to those of us in the advanced decades of life. When we find personal behavior in society shifting markedly (usually for the worse), the mores changing and attitudes and value judgements seemingly turned upside down, we find ourselves out of step and wondering what is this world coming to.

These changes vary greatly as to their significance, anywhere from the absence of ties and suit jackets on men attending churches these days to the growing number of "live-in" boyfriends and increasing acceptability of such sex before marriage behavior.

In a day when polls often drive political decisions and social surveys tend to describe acceptable attitudes and behavior in society, I find it difficult to sort out the changes which I am willing to accept and changes with which I cannot agree on moral grounds or for other reasons.

I have to ask my self, *at what points does my Christian faith commitment kick in and cause me to take a stand against the tide of change and popular opinion?* And if I take a stand against the grain of contemporary culture, does my stand apply only to my own behavior or do I feel an obligation to try and reverse what I believe to be a cultural slide into morally wrong behavior, or into mores which are hazardous and destructive for other reasons?

What is this world coming to, and what am I supposed to do about it?

–2010

SMALL IS COMFORTABLE

In Clinical Pastoral Education at Deaconess Hospital in Billings one time we were shown how to construct Genograms to use in counseling with people. It is a method of diagraming families and generations. The point of this exercise is to uncover relationships in the client's life which may have had an effect upon his or her his or her personality.

I think something similar has occurred in my self understanding through my writing down of memories from various stages in my life. I have discovered that repeatedly I have shied away from associating with large groups and have found small groupings much more comfortable

My high school had an enrollment of 3,800 students. I did not feel a part of this large group. For me my social context was the small high school youth fellowship in church. When I attended my 50th High School reunion the people I gravitated to were either from the church youth group or from my grade school class, which was relatively small.

After high school graduation I went to Urbana to begin the process of registering as a freshman at the University of Illinois, which was huge. Too large for me. I subsequently entered Elmhurst College which at that time had an enrollment of 290. And I enjoyed every minute of Elmhurst College.

After seminary when it came time to seek a call to my first position as an ordained minister I chose tiny Yoder and Hawk Springs in "tiny" Wyoming. No big city for me. I had always idealized living and working in a small town.

While Bozeman seemed big after our Wyoming residence, it still was comfortable in size, unlike Billings which was too big for me to feel a part of the total community In our early Billings years we visited Norm and Iris Austin in Forsyth frequently. I remember telling him that I envied him, in that the size of Forsyth was small enough to allow one to feel a part of the entire community .

I can see now that over the years small is comfortable for me.

–2010 at age 82

LOSING WHAT YOU NEVER HAD

Sorrow is generally associated with losing a person with whom one has been related for some time, or losing an object which has been in one's possession for a long time. We mourn the absence of what we once experienced with a person or an object.

But, it strikers me that there is another sort of mourning, It is mourning the loss of something one has never had. Perhaps an awareness of this kind of loss comes only in later years when all chance of having such an experience of a certain place or event, relationship or object is gone.

I mourn the fact that I shall never live in a little cottage for a month or two in a rural village in Scotland.

I mourn the fact that I shall never visit Vienna with its rich history of classical music.

I mourn the fact that I shall never tour the U.S. in an RV, going from place to place as "the spirit moves."

I mourn the fact that I never had a brother or a sister,.

I morn the fact that I shall never. . . .

–April 2010

CHALLENGED AND CHASTENED

After watching *The Diary of Anne Frank* on PBS a couple of nights ago I feel chastened for having held two opinions which have now been challenged. (1) I have faulted the Jewish people for keeping the Holocaust before our eyes continually after all these years with many museums and celebrations dedicated to keeping its memory vivid and alive. I have rather glibly thought *Why can't they forgive and forget?* (2) And I have grown in my commitment to pacifism, increasingly feeling that no war is justified.

Coincidentally, another event happened to me in the week before seeing the Anne Frank film. While visiting an old friend, Gerard Kuiper, who with his family emigrated from Holland to the U.S. shortly after World War II, he shared with me something of the extreme conditions his family was forced to experience during the Nazi occupation of Holland. He seriously affirmed to me his belief in the absolute necessity of ridding the world of Hitler and Naziism through military action.

Having thus been challenged and chastened, I think now that reviewing the Nazi cruelties will make us contemplate our own propensity for racist and ethnic cleansing in our own culture and time. Such remembering may very well be profoundly critical.

Furthermore I think I have been moved beyond a naive anti-war position to one which allows for military intervention as sometimes necessary to stem the tide of evil when other means have proven ineffective. However, instead of taking a "just war" position, it seems to me that my view point might be summed up in two seemingly opposing ideas: War as morally wrong but at times necessary.

At the very time Anne Frank was hiding in a stuffy attic in Amsterdam deprived of the freedom to go to school, I was blithely enjoying my high school years in complete freedom, totally unaffected by the scourge of evil enveloping Europe.

Anne Frank and Gerard Kuiper have chastened and challenged me to re-think my opinions on evil and war.

–May 2010

THREE SEE'S

How I want others to see me; how others see me, and how I see myself will always, I think, be to some extent differ. And I have an idea that the wider the differences the more troubled I will be. If, however, others see me pretty much the way I really am–the way I see myself–and if that is ok with me, then, I think, I will be pretty well adjusted.

We talk about another person as being "a very private person." Such persons seemingly do not want others to see them as they see themselves to any significant extent. This is also true of those who project a false facade. Such privacy or falsity may not be perceived by others as the person intends. The private person may be misunderstood as arrogant and aloof. Unless he or she is very good at it, the one playing a role may be seen false and insincere, as opaque as the quiet private person.

Three *see's*! If how each of us sees ourselves, projects ourselves and is seen by others are, quite close, we will be mentally healthy individuals.

–November 20, 2010

FOOTBALL AND TURKEYS

On the Friday before Thanksgiving turkeys and football, both of which are important elements in the American Thanksgiving Day celebration, were both in the local Bozeman news. A spokesperson for Montana State University announced that four million dollars had recently been contributed through the generosity of many donors toward a ten million dollar addition to the MSU football stadium which would be matched by the university, bringing the total so far to eight million. Another million in donations matched by MSU would complete the project so that the addition could be ready by football season 2011.

On the same day the local Bozeman Food Bank announced that 1200 families had requested food for a Thanksgiving meal and that only 180 turkeys had been given to the Food Bank to fulfill these wishes.

It strikes me that a lot of people who gave generously to the new stadium addition will have turkey with their football next Thursday, but hundreds of our neighbors will have only football (if their TV works) but no turkey on this coming Thanksgiving. This saddens me and makes me wonder about our society and its priorities.

And it impelled Doris and me to buy a twelve pound turkey and take it to the Food Bank on Saturday so that one more family in our town will have turkey on Thanksgiving--with or without football.

–December 2010

WHAT I DIDN'T WRITE

I am in the midst of writing notes to folks on our Christmas Card list. The annual mass letter is included, but I like to write something more personal on each one. In this season of joy, most of what we write each other is positive. How well the kids and grand kids are doing is especially popular.

However, as I have been writing, my mind has turned to what I am not writing–the negatives-the two losses in 2010.

The most recent was the totally unexpected and untimely death of my good friend, Jerry Crabs.

The other was the arrogant, self-righteous, and deceptive demise of the Spring Hill church, when the congregation was led by its pastors to forsake its Presbyterian U.S.A. heritage

I continue to mourn both of these losses.

–June 3 2011

WHAT IS IT ABOUT US?

The Associated Press reported in today's news that an auction conducted online brought about $190,000 from buyers who bid on the personal items from Ted Kaczynski's hide-away cabin in the mountains of Montana in 1996. Kaczynski was the so-called Unabomber who set off sixteen explosions across the country killing three persons and injuring twenty-three others in a crazed revolt against modern technological society. The fact that the money will go to assist the surviving families not withstanding, the despicable anti- social and violent actions of this one man, now in prison for life, are being celebrated and memorialized by lifting up for display this criminal's papers and possessions at a price of $190,000.

What is it about us that makes us want to glorify the evil doer's of society? Some years ago some of the most popular films were the series of Godfather stories about organized crime families.

Look at any paper-back book shelves in corner drug stores and you will find a sizeable proportion are murder mysteries or thrillers with violence on every other page. Television crime dramas retain high viewer ratings. Real-life murder, rape, assault and scandals make good press in print and electronic media. The public's appetite for war stories from our national past and current world wide news appears to be insatiable.

What is it about us?.

And then I have to admit the number of times I have boasted about a certain late night check in at the hotel I worked in when I was a bell-hop. Mrs. Frank Nitti, the widow of the late Frank Nitti, who took over the Capone mob after Al Capone was put in federal prison. Or the frequency with which I have been quick to tell people that I went to seminary in Chicago across the street from the Biograph Theater, where Elliot Ness finally shot and killed John Dillinger. I can even show you the telegraph pole in the alley where he was gunned down!

What is it about us?

–September 13, 2011

REDESIGNING THE HIGHWAY

All last week I wanted to say something about the continuing media hype before the tenth anniversary of 9/11. But I had mixed feelings--a conflict between the portrayal of the U.S. as innocent victim and wondering what we as a nation could have done differently in the past decades to discourage the threat of terror.

On Saturday, 9/10, a parable of sorts began to form in my mind:

There was once upon a time a very dangerous section of highway just outside a certain town. The highway skirted the edge of a very steep drop-off. Far too often vehicles driving this highway could not negotiate the curve and went over the side and plunged into the canyon, invariably causing serious injuries if not deaths. The town council considered the problem of the curving highway along the cliff and decided to put up guard rails. More than once the council re-installed higher guard rails in an attempt to keep people safe. This reduced the accident rate to some extent, but there were still tragic accidents due to this particular stretch of the highway. Then a new council member was elected and she had a radical idea, after seeing that the highway simply did not have enough bank in its design to slant vehicles away from the edge. As a result of her discovery the council redesigned the highway, and moved it inland a number of yards. After that there were no more plunges into the abyss.

Could it be, I wondered, that our ever increasing security measures are like the guard rail, and that what we need is to rethink our pathway through the international countryside?

I thought of the Old Testament prophets who often warned God's people of international danger lurking just beyond their borders and advised the nation to rethink the entire life of the nation and to begin again to try to live as God intended. That, however, was never easy for Israel; and this is even more difficult for us, I am afraid.

But I did not know if this is what I should say. Who was I to add my voice to the swelling tide of voices as 9/11 dawned?

And then on 9/11, during morning worship we sang some words which had been written especially for this day. These thoughts helped to resolve the conflict in my mind and led me beyond mere distress, to embrace a hope for a better world after 9/11. This, in part, is what we sang:

"Some sought to answer terror, the only way they knew–with anger toward the stranger and calls for vengeance, too. Yet this is not your answer, nor what you would create. May we live toward a future where love will conquer hate."

"God, give us faith and wisdom to be your healing hands; give open minds that listen to truth from all your lands. Give strength to work for justice; grant love that casts out fear Then peace and not destruction will be the victor here"

I guess this is nothing short of redesigning the highway.

–September 24, 2011

A HOUSE DESOLATE

The tide of illegal mind numbing drugs flowing into the U.S. across the border from Mexico is rising each year despite increasing futile attempts by border agents to stem the flow.

It is reported that one in five U.S. families with children do not have enough financial resources to feed their children adequately. Food banks across the country are finding that the number of hungry Americans seeking foods has doubled over the past year or so. But this is nothing compared to the hunger and starvation of thousands in war-torn nations in Africa.

All this against the backdrop of the appalling number of jobless Americans and the frightening number of home foreclosures which threaten the future of families all over the country.

And then there are those for whom hurricane, flood and earthquake continue to put their lives at serious risk, while disaster relief funds are running out.

At the same time we are pouring billions of dollars into the longest war in our history which General Petraeus said recently may well continue through our lifetime and that of our children.

I am sure these are only some of the stanzas in the tragic litany of current affairs which ought to concern us in our thoughts and prayers, and in our action.

When we look out across the world, I wonder if our words might be something like those which Jesus uttered when he approached Jerusalem on his way to the Cross?

"Jerusalem, Jerusalem, the city that kills the prophets and stones those who are sent to it! How often have I desired to gather your children together as a hen gathers her brood under her wings, and you are not willing. See, your house is left to you desolate." (Matthew 23:37,38)

–November 2011

FEAR, FREEDOM AND LOVE

In the novel which I have recently written, the two main characters in later life are unable to love each because of fear. When they were in high school they had no fear of each other and so were able to experience authentic love, at least as much as teenagers can. Now, after years of leading separate lives they have come together, but each is fearful of the other. Thus love cannot grow between them. In the story, Bob's fear of Joyce is driven by his guilt over having rejected and forsaken her earlier. The origin of Joyce's fear is to be found in the abuse her late husband had thrust upon her psychologically.

Fear and love are mutually exclusive. You can't have both in your relation to others. If one fears his or her spouse, love between them is thereby diminished.

On the other hand, the positive side of this is, that if there is true, selfless love between spouses, neither will fear the other.

This truth is enunciated in I John 4:18: *"There is no fear in love, but perfect love casts out fear; for fear has to do with punishment, and whoever fears has not reached perfect love."*

If one is fearful, one is not free to love. However, love has a way of liberating one from fear. Freedom and love dwell together. Fear and love do not!

And, by the way, I don't know yet whether Joyce and Bob will be able to love each other again. I don't know yet whether they will be able to be freed of their fear. I hope so, but their story is not yet over.

–December 9, 2011

7 C's SIX DECADES LATER

My thoughts tonight have been turned to the 7 C's, which was a devotional group seven of us in McCormick Seminary organized in the fall of 1949. In many ways it was one of the most significant aspects of my seminary years. And a most lasting set of relationships was given to us during those years and since. In the sixty years since seminary all but one of us have kept in touch, sharing with each other both our glad news and our anguish, as well as the more mundane aspects of our lives.

In today's mail was a Christmas card from one of the six, in which Bill Johnson, told of the death of his wife last May and of the death of his daughter two weeks later. Doris and I were brought up short by this news, for we were unaware of Shirley Johnson's death seven months ago, or of Linda's death soon after.

The bonds which have held us together since 1949 cause us to experience something of Bill Johnson's anguish. Not the first death among us, but the most recent.

And so, tonight I reflect upon our devotional group of long ago. When Seminary began for us we lived in McCormick Hall, a very old five story dormitory facing Halstead Street in the 2300 block, north. It has been razed since that time. One of us lived In Fowler Hall, also a vintage dormitory, close to the corner of Fullerton and Halstead.

Oscar Hussel and Bill Johnson were roommates, both from Cincinnati, Ohio. Chester Wetzel was from Cedar Rapids, Iowa, and Neal Perz was from Cleveland. Joe Degi from Canton, Ohio and I were roommates. I was from the Chicago area. And finally Bob Lodwick who lived in Fowler Hall was from Cincinnati. Thus the name-- *7 C's., each of us having come from a place whose name began with C.*

By graduation, or soon after, all of us were married. It was at about that time that we lost track of Neal. Thus the role call of our group was as follows:

Oscar and Shirley Hussel
Bill and Shirley Johnson
Chester and Margaret Wetzel
Joe and Sylvia Degi
Bob and Hedy Lodwick
Paul and Doris Krebill

Of these twelve, nine remain. Oscar, Shirley Johnson, and Chester have passed away, answering the roll call of the saints in heaven, as did two of the children in our families. Ross Krebill in 1960, and Linda Johnson in 2011.

It is my autumn reflection that in time we nine will join them in answering that roll call as well!

–May 2012

WHEN THE HOLE IS GREATER THAN THE REST OF IT.

When I was a boy in Chicago, I would often see heavy trucks rumbling by on hard rubber tires. These ancient vehicles and their drivers did not yet have the luxury of pneumatic tires on which one rides on air instead of iron-like rubber. When one looked at those wheels, the spokes spanned a distance from the hub much greater than they would with our of tires today. Thus one could say that the hole was larger than the width of the tire. . . the hole was greater than the rest of it. This made for a very bumpy ride for the driver and I would expect a very long work day indeed.

What can possibly be the point of all this? Some very delicious doughnuts have almost no hole at all. It's all made up of the good stuff. If a baker made doughnuts with their holes greater than the tasty part, sales would plummet, and the baker would despair, and his future would be bumpy at best.

All this leads us to a slogan used to cheer us up: *Look at the doughnut, not at the hole!* When one focuses on the hole and concentrates on what one does not have in the way of money, talents, friends, relationships, experiences, or any other so-called fulfillment, it's like riding on a flat tire. Life's journey becomes unbearably bumpy as one rides on the hard rubber of a flat tire in place of the air in a pneumatic tire.

So don't look at the hole, at what you do not have. Rather, look at the gifts you have and be buoyed up by the air in your tires, which, by the way, comes from God, if you take seriously the Biblical idea that the Holly Spirit is the *breath* of God upon our lives!

Then for you **THE WHOLE IS GREATER THAN THE PARTS.**

–May 2012

IS IT ME IN THE STORY?

Recently a fiction author is reported to have said that when you read a novel and it does not feel like the author is writing directly to you, put the novel down. It isn't worth reading. This is a criteria I will want to apply to novels which I will be reading, for I think this is a good standard.

Meanwhile this observation causes me to reflect upon my experience in reading novels, which may be close to what his author claims. Presently I am reading two different novels each of which produces a very different feeling in me after reading portions from it. The one leaves a "bad taste," so to speak, I feel depressed after reading many parts of it. The other lifts me to heights of inner happiness which are above the norm in my day to day life.

The first story is filled with naked ambition, deceit and treachery. In this story I feel as if I am the perpetrator and/or the victim of the sort of evil put forth in this novel.

The second story exudes thoughts and acts of love and honesty and the joyful responses these thoughts and actions bring forth.

As I think about this I believe that the operative word is identification. In each case the author is able to present a perceived reality into which I am drawn as I feel what it is like to be one or more of the characters in the story.

Perhaps this is what is meant by feeling as though the author is speaking directly to the reader. Or perhaps even more "directly about the reader. So when I ask *Is it really me in this story?* And if my answer is *Yes,* then it is a good novel!

A good story provides an illusion which transports the reader almost mystically into another life. How it feels to live in that "world" then is how it feels to the reader. And so it is, that some novels make me feel badly and others make me feel good, with many shades in-between.

Following the thought of the author whose comment got me started on this pathway, if the story doesn't provide me an adequate illusion of another reality, the book ought to be tossed out.

I wonder how my novels have scored in this regard. The closest responses which I can remember are those readers who told me that it felt to them as if the characters in the story were friends of theirs. So perhaps those readers at least felt as if the story was "me!"

–June 2012

PIETY: PUBLIC OR PRIVATE?

I have been wondering about specially called prayer times in the life of the church. I was involved in such prayer session called in order to seek God's help with a problem in one of the congregations in our Presbytery. Specifically, after attending that session I wonder if some of the verbalized praying in such meetings borders on what Jesus warns against in the opening verses of Matthew 6.

> *Beware of practicing your piety before others in order to be seen by them. . . Whenever you pray, do not be like the hypocrites, for they love to pray and stand and pray in the synagogues so that they may be seen by others. (Matthew 6: 1,5)*
>
> However Jesus taught: *Whenever you pray, go into your room and shut the door and pray to your Father whois in secret. (Matthew 6:6)*

The only conclusions I have a right to make concern my own participation in such events For me, then, praying publicly for help in my own personal spiritual struggles seems awkward and out of place, and for me does border on what Jesus warned us against.

–July 21, 2012

WHEN WILL WE EVER. . . . ?

Ever since early yesterday morning most of the TV channels have been filled with news, interviews, speeches, and commentaries on another mass shooting. This time in a movie theater in Aurora, Colorado. Twelve people were killed, fifty-eight injured, most of whom are still in the hospital. The lone gunman had a cache of guns of varying sizes, and thousands of rounds of ammunition–all legally purchased. And now, of course, we hear the shop-worn refrain: "It's not guns that kill, it's people." Well, the Aurora killer could not have slaughtered seventy people with his bare hands. When will we ever get over that misguided excuse?

Apart from the announcement of prayer vigils last night, and a few survivors testifying to the helpfulness of their faith, and God's saving grace in their own cases, I found no reference to a theological dimension of this condition of violence in our culture which has once again perpetrated a tragic massacre.

Psychologists have been made available to witnesses and survivors needing to work through this trauma. A number of psychologists have been interviewed in the media to help the listening audience process this horrific event. This, seems to me, is an attempt to "lift up with our bootstrap approach" to this troubling situation. It assumes that we have within each of us the resources to get through this nighmare.

I am not so sure we have it in us to cure this deadly cancer with which our society is afflicted. Might this be a time for us as a society to take down the wall we have erected to keep God out of national life?

To put it more accurately, is this not a time to open our eyes to see what God is doing and to try and comprehend what God wants for our nation and our world? When will we ever learn to think theologically as we consider domestic and world affairs?

Might there be a Voice other than that of the N.RA.? When will we ever learn to listen?

–July 2012

HUMANS: MORE OF THE SAME OR DIFFERENT?

A recent thoughtful response to my blog on gun violence in Colorado opened with this observation:

> *Human animals, like other species, have the propensity for violence. That propensity can be diminished or enhanced by 'environmental' (read 'cultural') factors.*

I find myself in agreement with this assertion, but I am uncomfortable with what I see as implied limits upon the capacity of the human will to depart from the culturally imposed course of behavior.

This, I think, begs these basic questions: *(1) As humans are we merely quantitatively more than the "lower creatures?" (2) Or are we qualitatively different from other species?*

If the answer to the first is YES, then changes in our behavior either for more violence, or for reducing violence, will depend only upon environmental or cultural conditioning. If the answer to the second question is YES, then we will have the capacity to make changes despite or contrary to cultural conditioning.

–August 2012

THE PAST RUSTS IN TODAY'S WEEDS

Ever since the early 50s when Orville and Sylvia Lanham took us to Castle, a ghost town near Martinsdale, Montana, we have been intrigued by these towns of the past which are rusting and rotting in the weeds of time. Our favorite was Elkhor in Jefferson County with its stately Fraternity Hall beside what we always thought was a hotel.

This past week Doris and I took Marilyn and Kevin Brock, old time friends from Illinois, to visit Elkhorn. Once again it is the intermingling of past and present which intrigues me. When we entered the town, we parked our 2004 Chrysler next to a weed patch out of which protruded the rusting remains of an unidentifiable coupe of the 1920's.

In a curious way this collision of past and present is especially true of Elkhorn, for many of the old houses are being refurbished to accommodate modern day residents. As one stands in the doorway of the Fraternity Hall, one can almost "see" the little graduation class on the stage with their proud parents sitting before them in seats on the main floor, or a crowd of miners and their spouses applauding a theatrical performance of a traveling troupe of actors. And now outside along the gravel street, a modern SUV rushes by loaded with groceries and a family headed for their summer home up the street. Their house has new windows and doors recently installed in the ancient log and frame walls erected over a hundred years ago.

The swirling weeds through which Kevin walks to take digital photos of a collapsing shed, reveal the almost buried rusting artifacts used by former residents of a once thriving Elkhorn.

I remember another poignant scene from elsewhere in Montana when we came upon the empty site of former farm house. Next to where its front entrance had once been, there blazed in the summer sun the rich purple blossoms of a mature lilac bush.

Yes, the *past* is *present* as it rusts and rots in today's weed and flowers.

So with our lives! What we have experienced is part of our every breathing moment now!

–September 2012

THE POWER OF FICTION TO INFUSE

Ever since I retired in the fall of 1992, I have been reading fiction–one novel after another. I've had no formal education in the reading or writing of fiction. My selection has usually been quite random. Earlier, many of these were classics from nineteenth-century English writers. But for the most part these have been of a more contemporary and popular nature. But most of these I would call serious, in that they seek to depict authentic human situations, not contrived to sell.

Throughout my reading I have been struck by the power of the novel to transport the reader into the life of another person, namely a fictional figure in the story In many cases it is as if I have been made to become the character in the story I am reading, to see what he or she hears, to feel what he or she feels. To *be* that person. It is the power of good fiction to infuse another life into the very consciousness of the reader.

I have been reading a novel by a relatively unknown author who has given me the opportunity to live some experiences which I myself have not had, thereby expanding my life significantly. In this story the main character is a man in his forties who has lost his beloved wife to a sudden blood clot, leaving him with an infant son. This happened a few months after their teenage daughter had rejected her family and had run off with a man who despised her parents.

Through this work of fiction I now have experienced this double loss, and know how that feels more fully than any objective description of such a situation could have provided. In my imagination my life has been temporarily infused with the life of another person.

For me, this is the power of fiction in my life to help me see and feel through another person's sensitivity.

–September 2012

MORE ABOUT FICTION

I sometimes wonder if wishful thinking lies behind what novelists envision with rose-colored glasses in the stories they give us. It is one thing to set one's story in a delightful place in which the novelists would like to be, but quite another matter to pose a level of delight in human relationships which rarely, if ever exist. The setting imagined may very well be realistically described, but some of the interpersonal interactions seem to me to be so idealized that I believe they are the result of wishful thinking on the part of the novelist which the reader then enjoys. This, I believe is a violation of one of the rules by which I try to write fiction. I believe that the story and its characters should be to be true to life, real people making plausible decisions in the face of real life situations.

–September 16, 2012

UNLIKELY? NOT LIKELY!

Today's Sunday edition of the Bozeman Chronicle has a feature article on what it calls "a seemingly unlikely alliance" of three local clergy "to bring the community educational, and spiritual experiences and to participate in social justice activities."

From what I read in the article I find myself in agreement with what they intend to discuss and do. It is in full agreement with what my own Christian tradition deems a necessary aspect of our mission. What I take issue with is the Chronicle's assertion that this alliance is "unlikely."

We have already in Montana a much broader coalition of clergy and churches of religious traditions joined together in the Montana Association of Churches, which, among other worthwhile emphases, is putting forth education and action on social justice issues.

Furthermore, I find this particular alliance much more likely than unlikely from a theological perspective. I have long seen a great deal of commonality among many adherents of the Reformed Jewish, Unitarian Universalist and progressive Congregational persuasions, especially in regard to their rejection of the concept of the incarnation i.e. the divinity of Christ.

–September 2012

WHAT'S ALL THE SHOOTIN' ABOUT?

Mass protests and acts of violence have broken out in the Arab and Muslim world over a film made in the U.S. which denigrates the Prophet Muhammad who is sacred to those of the Muslim faith. In the politicizing efforts to explain what is going on, some have linked the violence to a previously planned attack on the U.S. on the anniversary of the 9/11 attack. Others have tried to minimize the influence of the film in one way or another.

I think this film, as well as the response to it in the Islamic world and in our country, is an unanticipated result from two of our basic freedoms. While the U.S. government has condemned the film and declares that it does not represent the thinking of the majority of Americans, all of us recognize that freedom of expression has permitted this film to be made and distributed, even though most of us wish otherwise.

Furthermore, it seems to me, that an unintended result of our basic tenet of freedom of religion has been to make us unaware of the depth of religious sensibilities in the Islamic world which this film has violated. Thus, some of us have passed off this widespread reaction at the gates of our embassies and in the streets as that of extremists. Otherwise we wonder "what all the shootin's about.

Freedom of religion for Americans means appropriately–-the separation of church and state. I believe that an unintended and unanticipated result of this separation doctrine has been the departure of religion from public discourse, and its movement to the periphery of the important concerns in society. With this mind-set we wonder why anyone should get so upset about a film which denigrates a religious figure in anybody's religion. Could it be that we do not understand the widespread feeling in the Arab world for its sacred Prophet? Perhaps we have lost sight of the sacred in our national consciousness as well. So, again we wonder "what's all the shootin' about.'"

However, a positive result of the freedom of religion concept is the development of respect and tolerance of the religious commitments of others, a reverence for the sacred wherever it is to be found.

This should produce an attribute among all of us which would restrain us from saying or filming anything offensive to the religious feelings of others even though we have the freedom to do so. Then there might not be so much "shootin'" in the world.

–November 2012

A GLASS OF COOL WATER

I am finally learning to understand and embrace what Dr. Davies, our New Testament professor in seminary many years ago, meant when he revealed something of his own personal faith. When asked to tell us something of his own personal experience of life and of God's grace, he spoke of his appreciation for a "glass of cool water" as an example of his own joy in life.

At the time, none of us seemed to be able to relate to what he was saying. In fact he seemed embarrassingly simple, if not naive. I was twenty-five years old at the time when Dr. Davies words were ingrained in my consciousness. Now sixty years later, this morning Dr. Davies' personal revelation came alive to me with new meaning and with a feeling I now also am beginning to share.

This way of looking at day to day life came clear to me when I read a passage in *The Deepest Waters,* a novel by Dan Walsh about a pre- Civil War voyage.

Laura has been rescued from a sinking steamship and brought aboard a sailing ship. She is desolate because her husband of a few months had to be left behind. Micah, a black slave, who works aboard the sailing ship tries to comfort Laura by telling her how he has survived the loss of his family as well as numerous cruel beatings, by sharing with her how he does not look backward or forward, taking only one day at a time. Certainly not a new or a profound thought, but one which helps Laura through some very trying times.

And so, following both Micah and Dr. Davies, I will try to dwell upon the joys of the moment instead of upon what might be seen as unfortunate circumstances of the past or a certain uneasiness about the future.

At this point my "glass of cool water" is the hour I spend alone in a local café with a cup of coffee, a raisin cookie and a novel I'm reading, or the hour at the coffee house with Max and Lowell sharing thoughts personal or profound, the warm cozy feeling of my pillow when I first climb under the covers each night, an egg salad sandwich with Doris along a road in Yellowstone, or the caramel nut roll from Wheat Montana we share as we return to the road. These are a few of the simple pleasures which refresh the day I am living at the time.

Thank you, Dr. Davies. Thank you, Micah.

–November 2012

YOU CAN'T GO HOME AGAIN

Under Jody's leadership we are studying Timothy Keller's The Prodigal God, which is a very insightful exploration of the full meaning of the parable of the prodigal son. As he talks about the son's ultimate desire to return home Keller refers to a universal desire of all of us to return to the place from which we have come which we idealize in our memory. But if we return we don't find it as we had remembered it. This has gotten me to thinking about what places of my childhood are like that. Sadly, I do not look back at the houses or apartments in which I lived as child in quite that way. I wonder why.

I remember very little of the apartment in Chicago in which my parents and I lived from my second year until I was in first grade. No particular experiences come to mind except of my having hidden from company behind a couch in the living room. I remember being with children who lived in a flat in a two story building next door and walking with my parents around the block or to the nearby grade school.

The only separate house in which we lived was on Marion Street in Oak Park from second grade to the first months of high school. Again, not much comes to mind in the way of nostalgic memories of living in that house. But many experiences of playing with kids on our block remain in my memory.

The third and final residence was the first floor of a two flat building on a busy street in Oak Park quite far from the house on Marion Street. I remember the rooms, eating meals with my parents in the kitchen or dining room, playing by myself on the floor in the living room while my parents read, doing my homework at my desk in the spare bedroom, but not much else. No contact with anyone else on the block, except occasionally with the single man upstairs.

I do not have any desire to go back to any of these places. However I did have a desire to go back to my grandparents' house in Iowa, which held vivid memories for me. But in recent years when my uncle, Harvey, took Doris and me to see that house, it was a huge disappointment for me. In many ways all that I idealized in my memory was gone. The house was cluttered and in disrepair and depressing to me.

This proves to me the cliche, "You can't go home again." To the houses of my childhood, that is.

Instead, my memories seem to involve activities with playmates, many rides with my parents around the Chicago area, and Horace Mann grade school and Oak Park High School. Most all of these memories are happy ones.

A DUMB IDEA

The novel, *The Life of Pi,* and subsequently the movie, leaves the reader, or the viewer, with the question, "Was that something which really happened?"

In my own effort to put a rational explanation on the story, I have an idea that the story of the tiger and the boy named Pi in a life boat after a shipwreck in the middle of the ocean is a dream which Pi had during those terrible survival days in the ocean–the sort of a dream which comes when one is delirious. Earlier, his father had cautioned Pi very strongly not to have anything to do with the dangerous tiger in the zoo, when, in fact, Pi wanted very much to relate to the animal. That, I think, was the kernel of truth with which Pi struggled in his dream.

The second story, which Pi told to the reporters who didn't believe the first story, I think, also was a dream Pi had during his ordeal in the ocean. This one came from his confrontation with the cook on the ship, who becomes the villain in the dream.

When I shared this theory with those with whom I had seen the film, I was met with no comment. I took this to mean either disagreement or that mine was a dumb idea, most likely the latter. Oh well, life goes on. I needn't be concerned about tigers or shipwrecks, even if it might not have been a dream.

–December 2012

WITH GUNS UNDER THEIR BATHROBES

"Christmas came early for law-abiding gun owners. . ." So said Illinois state representative, Brandon Phelps, as he rejoiced over the recent decision the 7th U.S. Circuit Court of Appeals to strike down the Illinois ban on concealed weapons.

(As reported in today's Bozeman Daily Chronicle)

That means that now in not-so-peaceful Chicago at the next Christmas pageant you plan to attend, watch out! Those innocent looking Wise Men coming to pay homage to the baby Jesus, born the Prince of Peace, may well have guns concealed under their bath robes.

Christmas which came early, as Phelps proclaimed, could be your last if you attend the wrong pageant. Not a good definition of Christmas early or late I'd say.

–December 12, 2012

SLAM DUNK

I have found that nothing kills the chance of a good and satisfying conversation so much as a slam dunk. This lethal reply can take many forms. When one offers an opening comment, idea, or opinion only to be told that it is ridiculous to ever think such a thing, the chance of conversation on the matter presented is considerably diminished.

When one states something and is immediately forcefully corrected with what the truth really is, either an argument will ensue, or the corrected one will concede the point and subsequently have little more to say on the matter, or worse yet, nothing to say on any other subject.

A proclamation of a moral judgment upon a person or situation introduced into the discussion will often bring a conversation to a sudden halt, implying that nothing more can be said to redeem the situation.

Perhaps the most deadly response to an initial contribution to an anticipated discussion is to be ignored, while some other subject is pursued instead of what one has suggested for discussion.

In all such cases–*slam dunk*–no more to be said.

We decry the loss of good conversationalists. I wonder if the slam dunk might be at least part of the reason for the demise of satisfying and stimulating conversation.

–December 2012

IS THAT YOU?

A much appreciated Christmas card from my cousin brought me her question which has arisen while reading my novel, *WESTBOUND*–a form of "Is that you?" She is wondering if the experience of the Rev. Earl Norris coming to Saline, Montana, in the novel is really the story of my coming from Chicago as a young clergy person to become the pastor of two small congregations in rural Wyoming in the 1950s.

Well, the answer is "Yes" and "No." My wife happily accompanied me to Hawk Springs and Yoder, Wyoming, and in many ways became "the perfect minister's wife." Earl's fiance' left him when he decided to become a minister.

But the lure of the West which motivated Earl to come to Montana and to remain in the West was also my inspiration in coming west to Wyoming and Montana after having grown up, as Earl did, in a suburb of Chicago. Subsequently the cultural differences which Earl felt were the ones I felt as well.

And so all along the way in *WESTBOUND* there will be experiences and feelings which Earl and I share both from our Chicago days and from later times in the West, and in New Zealand as well. However, the plot line in Earl's story is much different from my storyline.

I first discovered the question of whether a novel of mine is autobiographical after a long time friend and associate read my first novel, *FAIRHAVENS,* also featuring a young minister. However in this story Max and his wife are not happy in a small Montana congregation in which Max is the pastor. The friend who had been the church secretary in our Billings congregation for many years, and who was aware of my Wyoming pastorate was quite concerned when she told me, "I didn't know you were so unhappy in your first pastorate!"

Again this called for a mixed answer. Doris and I were very happy in Wyoming. Max and Gwen were not. And yet the two settings were very similar. And as *FAIRHAVENS* progressed, a number of places in the story would come from my own experience but the situations taking place in them for Max would be very different from mine.

And so also with the other novels, even though they do not concern a clergyperson there are autobiographical aspects in the midst of stories very divergent from mine.

Is it me? YES and NO.

–January 2013

SCARY BEDFELLOWS

It looks like a monumental fight is brewing over so-called gun control. On the one side are those who believe that gun violence must at all cost be curbed. This position is strongly opposed by advocates of Second Amendment rights, who assert that any governmental intervention in the free access to firearms is a dangerous limitation of the freedom to bear firearms under the constitution, which reads:

> *A well regulated Militia, being necessary to the security of a free State, the right of the people to keep and bear Arms, shall not be infringed as in the Second Amendment.*

I heard two statements on the subject recently on television news, which taken together, are quite disturbing, I think. One was a commentary in which the informal coalition of three movements was described: The gun lobby, the Christian Right, and the Tea Party

One of the defining similarities of these groups is the often quoted slogan from Ronald Reagan. "The government is the problem." The Tea Party complains that the government is stealing our money from us through taxation. The Gun Lobby believes that the government is scheming to take away our guns. And the Christian Right blames the government for taking the Christian religion and morality out of American life. In all three of these cases the government is seen as robbing us of our way of life and freedom as set forth in the Constitution.

Even more disturbing was an interview with a supporter of the N.R.A. anti-government stance, who said that the assault rifle should not be banned because such a weapon would be needed if one had to oppose government troops. Such talk is terrifying, if not treasonous.

The Christian Right and the Tea Party want to remove government meddling in their freedoms and their particular points of view. And the extremist gun advocates want to be ready to remove the government from our lives completely. We have seen examples of this in the past. Consider the anti-government stand-off of the Freemen movement at Jordan, Montana in 1996.

Taken to the extreme, these three bedfellows would bring us to a state of anarchy, the definition of which is "the absence of political authority." The anarchy here lurks behind the Second Amendment shield of Constitutional respectability. This is scary, especially so when at least one of the groups is convinced that God is exclusively on its side.

–February 2013

"COMPLETE SURRENDER"

I have been pondering the movie, *Chariots of Fire* and our discussion at church of its message. Eric Liddell's refusal to run on Sunday, regardless of the importance of the race, is the centerpiece of the story. The most obvious issues raised in the film are those of Sabbath keeping and the broader question of taking a stand against the claims of one's own culture culture when such claims conflict with ones religious commitments.

Underlying these particular events in Liddell's life is the concept of commitment, or in Liddell's own words, *surrender.*

As a Christian missionary in China, Liddell, along with many of his fellow missionaries, was thrown into an internment camp by the Japanese during the invasion of China by Japan in 1943. He died two years later of a brain tumor while still in the camp. A fellow missionary reported that Eric's last words were "It's complete surrender."

Liddell's complete surrender to God, his foremost and only commitment, was, I think, the message of the film and of his life.

In the scene in which he is brought before the British Olympic committee, including the Prince of Wales, Liddell's complete surrender to God is challenged by the British leaders, who want him to give his ultimate loyalty to his country instead of to God.

Also in contrast to Eric's complete surrender to God is what appears to me to be Liddell's competitor, Harold Abrahams' compulsive need not only to justify his place in society but to exalt himself above others.

Surrendering one's will to God's intention for us is, I believe, the basic message of the film and of Eric Liddell's entire life.

As he said, "It's complete surrender."

–March 2013

ALL IS WELL–ALL WILL BE WELL

A couple of weeks ago we saw Linda Loving's performance of Julian of Norwich, the 14th century Christian mystic and spiritual advisor. I had seen this twice before, but apparently this time I was ready and needful for the insight which Julian provided. For me the climax of her teaching came at the end of this particular dramatic presentation. I cannot remember the exact phrase but the overwhelming sense was that God loves us. I know that this certainly is not new information, but this time "I got it!"

Among other considerations of this insight I remembered hearing that Karl Barth, the important Reformed theologian of post-war Europe, was asked what he thought was the most important Christian message. His answer was to quote the first line of the familiar old hymn: *Jesus loves me, this I know, for the Bible tells me so.* This for me is a validation of my personal response to Julian's declaration.

As a result I have become able to affirm that the most important fact of life for me is that God loves me. God's love for me brings me God's forgiveness, the comfort of his guidance and protection–and much, much more. The words of the King James version of Psalm 23 become very relevant to me: *Thy rod and thy staff, they comfort me.*

Thus the words of Julian to her neighbors are becoming my assurance as well: *All is well-- All will be well.* Furthermore, I have now begun to experience what I have known intellectually. That when I feel so profoundly God's love for me, I am made more able to love others more fully despite whatever faults they may have. Such a re-orientation does not happen "overnight" but gradually as one allows God's love to permeate one's attitudes toward others.

Again: *All is well-- All will be well.*

–June 2013

SUPERANNUATED

The first time I came across this term: "superannuated" was in New Zealand, where this was the word used for the older adults in the population, all of whom were eligible for some form of retirement pension from the government. At the time I didn't think much about the term. But lately, now that my age qualifies me for such a designation, I have had cause to wonder about the term and whether I was experiencing this condition. One definition which I read for this word was "ineffective because of advanced age. . . outmoded. . . obsolete."

Now I wonder. *Have I become ineffective? Do others regard me As outmoded and obsolete?* I have known of retired clergy who are quite unhappy because they are not being given any meaningful opportunities for service or participation in the church they attend in retirement.

I remember Jesse Halsey, our pastoral theology professor in seminary, who had retired from a long ministry in a downtown church in Cincinnati. In a very earnest and pleading way he said to us. "If there is a older retired pastor in your congregation, invite him to give the benediction once in a while." At the time I did not understand the significance of such an extended hand to a superannuated pastor. Now I understand.

–October 2013

BIRDS OF A FEATHER

It's nice to read something which backs up what you have been saying all along. I have thought and said for some time that there is a similarity in the theological positions of some traditional Congregationalists, Unitarians and liberal Jews, particularly in their view of Jesus as neither divine nor set apart from the rest of .humanity in any substantive way. On this critical belief, I think many in the Congregational, Unitarian, and Jewish traditions tend to have a high level of agreement.

And so I was very interested to pick up a brochure advertising a public forum dealing with violence in our culture sponsored by the Congregation Beth Shalom, Pilgrim Congregational UCC, and the Unitarian Universalist Fellowship of Bozeman, featuring the following three "Faith Leaders:" Rabbi Ed Stafman of Congregation Beth Shalom, Rev. Glover Wagner of Pilgrim Congregational UCC, and Rev. Dr. Nina Gray of the Unitarian Universalist Fellowship.

This forum is one of a number of programs under The Power of We, an interfaith collaboration of the three religious organizations mentioned above.

Lest one concludes that these are only three religious groups in Bozeman concerned with violence in our culture, it should be noted that most Christian churches and faith leaders have a similar concern.

No, my observation has to do with issue of the nature of Jesus Christ and how these three *birds of a feather stick together.*

–November 2013

THE M. & M. OF TRAGEDIES

It would seem that barely a week goes by without another fatal shooting. This week it was at LAX. True to form the media tells us what they can about the **Method** before going onto a much more extensive reporting of the **Motive.** The shooting at the Los Angeles Airport terminal, we were told, was with an assault rifle which the killer took out of bag and began spraying death as he shot his way into the secure area.

So much for the method. Next we want to know the motive. We are uneasy without knowing the motive. Then, when we are finally told what the killer's motive was it is as if we can then rest back with a sigh of relief and say to ourselves. "Oh, that explains it." *–case closed–* until next week when there may very well be another killer, with another firearm and another motive.

There are some serious dangers, I think, in our customary responses to these kinds of violent lethal acts done by our fellow citizens. (1) Confusion by which we make an explanation to be an excuse. Such consuming preoccupations as hatred of the federal government, hurt over some domestic injustice, a seething resentment against another person or group, or other such motive may well explain why a person has murdered another human being, but these explanations must not be understood as excuses or justification by any stretch of the imagination.

(2) Failure to examine critically the method by which slaughter is being thrust upon the public or upon selected individuals. Out of fear of reprisal, I believe we have been seduced into accepting the various elements of the "gun lobby" and their slick excuses: slogans such as

It's not guns that kill, it's people. Yes, but I'd a whole lot rather be in an airport where there is a guy wielding a box cutter than one with an AK 47.

After all, we are a nation of game hunters. That may be, but I wish hunting would be the only reason people have guns.

Beware of violating the second amendment. Yes, yes, I am glad that the police force, the armed forces, the National Guard and security personnel have guns to protect us and our freedom but Joe Blow next door, our children's teachers, or the kid in a drive by my shooting –that's another matter, needing some serious consideration, I think

Having a gun makes you and your family more safe. I'm not so sure. Who's to say that you'll be able to get the gun out, cocked and aimed in time to save your neck. It would be a whole lot better to call 911. What about the little kid who comes to your door to sell something, and you get terrified by such an intrusion and you shoot the poor child.

(3) Perhaps the most insidious danger is our becoming immune to the horror of death by firearms. *Could it be that we see so much carnage in war-torn places of the world and on the streets and campuses of our own land that we no longer flinch at the sight of such blood?* I hope not! The death of one human being, no matter to whom or where such a tragic event occurs, ought to be as excruciatingly painful as the death of one's closest loved one or ones' own death. Indiscriminate

Let us not waiver in our attention to both the **M. & M.'s** of tragedies which are occurring with alarming frequency. Much must be done to help people deal with their lethal **MOTIVES** in order to avert violent results. And we must no longer turn a blind eye to the indiscriminate ownership and use of firearms as the **METHOD** violent yearnings are carried out.

–November 2013

COPERNICUS AGAIN

In 1543 Nicolaus Copernicus, a Polish mathematician and astronomer, published his findings that the Earth was not the center of the universe, but rather this key position was now to be given to the Sun This heliocentric view of the universe was contrary to the teaching of the Christian religion. Eventually, after the death of Copernicus the Catholic Church banned the book Copernicus had written in which he had set forth his conviction that the Earth was not the center of the universe, thus denying the select position of our planet. Now Copernicus' view is accepted universally. So far as I am aware, even the Biblical literalists who deny the concept of evolution accept the heliocentric model in which the sun is the center of our solar system.

Well, "Copernicus" is at it again! The Associated Press has recently reported that NASA data has been used by astronomers to calculate that in our galaxy "there are at least 8.8 billion stars with earth-size planets in the habitable temperature zone." These findings strengthen the theory of many astronomers, as well as that of many in the general public, that there is life elsewhere in the universe, and the resulting conjecture that "we are not alone," that there is intelligent life elsewhere in the universe

Strangely, I find myself in a position a bit similar to those who opposed Copernicus. He had taken away the central place of the earth. And that was contrary to their Christian belief. I do not oppose the scientific evidence which supports the idea that there is or has been life on other planets. But I take issue with the tacit assumption that if there is life, then it follows that human, intelligent life no doubt will have evolved. This position, I think, develops from the commonly held opinion in the scientific community that human life is merely quantitatively related to "lower" species. Such ideas as the belief that our brains are merely more complex and larger than that of other primates seem to me to say that there is no qualitative difference between us and other creatures. This view I believe, is contrary to the Christian theological view of the human being as created in the image of God, a little less than God, according to the Psalmist.

I am not a Biblical literalist, but the concept of humanity as not just an extension of the rest of nature, but rather as particularly created by God, is a belief which I hold as a Christian.

I believe we have not evolved in the image of an ape. We have been created in the image of God. Thus, whether or not we are alone in the universe is not due merely to favorable conditions on other planets. It is up to God, and not subject to our scientific investigation or conjecture.

And by way of a disclaimer of sorts, I haven't found anyone–family or friend–who agrees with me on this!

–January 2014

"FADING MORAL UNDERPINNING"

I must confess that I do not regularly read Letters to the Editor in our local newspaper. But this past week a pair of such letters struck my eye. Each was written by a friend of mine in my church. The first letter was from a high school senior, recently recovered from the devastation of having been caught in the undertow of a rampant drug culture here and throughout the nation. The earnest heartfelt thrust of his letter to his community is that we must face up to the problem of widespread use of mind-altering chemicals and reverse "this never-ending spiral of neglect that will destroy our youth."

The second letter appearing a few days later was written by a retired insurance executive and leader in church circles here and nationally. In his letter he takes on the challenge issued by the younger correspondent to try to "do something to halt this abysmal slide," which he identifies as due to our "fading moral underpinning."

The clue, I think, to our social slide into moral chaos and to what we must due to reverse his "spiral of neglect," lies in the word ***underpinning.*** This is an architectural engineering term used as a metaphor. The underpinning is the foundational structure placed on a solid immovable footing such a rock, upon which a building will stand sturdiy and safely. Without such an underpinning the structure will be in danger of eventual collapse.

This metaphor points to the need for a society to be founded upon solid, immovable, undisputed moral teachings. And it predicts the ultimate collapse of a society in which there is little agreement as to what is right and appropriate behavior or as to what is not right.

Like the rock lying beneath the building which supports its underpinning, so the moral principles upon which the underpinnings of a healthy society depend must originate from beyond the society itself.

In my opinion our society often replaces the solid rock from outside the structure of society for its foundation, with the shifting sands of whatever it is each of us thinks is right for him or herself as the source of society's behavior.

The solid rock to which I refer is God's will and intention for humankind. A society founded upon such divine source of authority will have a chance of surviving.

In place of the will of a divine authority as the basis for our actions it seems that we would rather base our behavior upon what we want or upon what the crowd wants us to do. This way of living is based upon the shifting sands of human wants and wishes.

Thus, to a dangerous extent we have become a society without adequate underpinnings, one which instead is spread upon shifting sands, and which will finally collapse upon itself, it seems to me.

This is what I believe is described by my friend in his letter as "our fading moral underpinning."

But, "The society which hears these words of mine and does them will be wise for having built itself upon the rock; and the rain fell and the floods came and the winds blew and beat upon it, but it did not fall, because it had been founded on the rock." (Paraphrase of Matthew 7:24,25)

–January 21, 2014

WHERE ARE THE OTHER 70 MINUTES?

I found the short segment on NBC's TODAY SHOW disappointing and disconcerting, this morning. It featured two of our local heroes: Tom Brokaw, retired NBC Anchor who now lives down the road near Big Timber, and Greg Mortenson, Bozeman based author of Three Cups of Tea and builder of schools in central Asia, mainly for girls. The Today Show featured five minutes or less of a seventy-five minute interview of Mortenson by Brokaw taped earlier and out of earshot of the public.

The part of the interview we were privileged to see focused upon questions of the veracity of his book, upon criticism lodged against Mortenson for his mishandling of funds, and how he feels about these negative responses to his work This coverage, I think, has left the audience with the impression that the efforts of Mortenson to build schools in Asia are now considerably diminished.

Sadly, nothing was said about the reorganization of the Central Asia Institute, founded by Mortenson, to more responsibly handle its funds and accountability. Nothing was said about Mortenson's continuing productive activity in Central Asia to build schools for children, particularly for girls who otherwise would remain unschooled.

I do not fault Tom Brokaw for Today Show's selection of the gory details of allegations made against Greg instead of the glory of what Mortenson and the CAI are doing as a creative alternative to war and violence in that part of the world. It would seem that the quality of media coverage has been trumped by the attempt to gain a higher quantity of viewers.

Where are the seventy minutes which we did not see? Covered up by the media's "bottom line," in my opinion.

–February 2014

MYSTICAL POWER OF FICTION

In my experience some novels have a mystical power to put the reader into the shoes of its characters, thus imparting to the reader the emotions of the characters involved. My most recent experience of this has come about in my reading of one of Beverly Lewis's novels in which she tells of the lives of Old Order Amish folk in Lancaster County, Pennsylvania.

In this group the rules for courting are strict and clearly known. Caleb is courting Nellie under these rules which have been determined by the Bishop and are enforced by his father. When they are caught "red handed" having pushed the boundaries slightly over the proclaimed limits, the two young people are mortified and guilt-ridden when confronted by Caleb's father. After reading this portion of the story I found myself similarly mortified, even though rationally I knew that I had never been in such a position. Once again I experienced the power of fiction to project vicariously the emotions of its characters upon my consciousness.

This transference is not confined to negative disturbing emotions. Joy and happiness as well as other moods and dispositions can also flood our consciousness when we read passages permeated with such emotions.

–February 2014

WHAT IN THE WORLD IS THE SOUL?

Well, to begin with, I don't think it is in the world. Perhaps it is the ultimate musing to try and say what the soul is. Let me try to muse!

I don't think the soul is a thing. It is not some sort of see-through layer floating around one's body. It does not occupy a place in space or time. It is not even a capacity which one may or may not possess to a varying extent.

My sense of the soul is that it is the "I" in one's own consciousness. Apart from all input from outside oneself, when one's thoughts subside, and only one's own self is present, there remains down deep in one's consciousness, the "I" –my essence as human being, the overriding feeling of that I AM. It is what is meant by self consciousness. And this does not change over time. After my eighty-six years, I am the same "me" as my earliest memories would reveal. Soul is timeless, eternal, not altered by the death of body and mind.

Soul, I think, is a distinctly human essence, present in every human being to the same extent, but not present in any other creatures. Soul is not a product of the evolutionary process. "I AM" is an awareness none other in all creation possesses.

To use traditional Christian theological language, the soul is the image of God conferred upon each human being. In the Biblical story of Moses' confrontation with God, Moses asks the identity of God and God's answer is ***"I AM."*** This gift from God of self-awareness is what I believe is SOUL. Timeless and eternal, I expect my Soul's self awareness to continue after my death.

The thought of Augustine, I think, pertains to the Soul. "Thou hast made us for thyself, O Lord, and our heart (soul)is restless until it finds its rest in thee."

–February 2014

COFFERS INSTEAD OF POLLS

There is a lot of talk these days about early voting as a means of enfranchising more voters, which is good for our democracy. But there is another early voting which is bad for our democracy. That is voting at the coffers for your preferred candidate long before the rest of us go to the polls. Montana has had its one U.S. Representative in Washington for his first two years. He announced lately that he is running for the Senate in 2016.

With minimal experience he may just win the vote because of the number of people who have already voted for him by going to his coffers with their money. Thus he already has millions more dollars in his coffers than the others who plan to run against him have in their coffers. Yes, the voting has begun and the new slogan is "May the one with the most money in his coffers win." This slogan has replaced the traditional slogan of our democracy which has been "May the best person win." Similarly the polls as the traditional place to vote has been replaced with the new place to vote-- at the coffers of your candidate of choice. Is it any wonder that the polls are not as busy as they once were?

–March 8, 2014

HOLY MEANS WHOLLY SEPARATE

It was reported by Associated Press that one of the speakers at the Conservative Political Action Committee annual conference had this to say about God. "If this nation forgets our God, then God will have every right to forget us." While the first half of this proclamation may very well point to the failure in the recognition of God by many of us in today's society, it is offensive and just plain wrong to imply that God has the human weakness of forgetting. And furthermore it is audacious to presume to grant God the human attribute of rights to do anything or to refrain from anything.

I realize that the speaker was making a political statement and not attempting a theological affirmation. However, sloppy theology in the service of partisan politics could be one of the factors which makes many in our society decide to forget God. For who wants a god who forgets and whose rights are determined by what we as a nation do or don't do?

In the Hebrew and Christian faith traditions God is perceived as HOLY. That is to say that God is entirely separate from God's creation, including humankind, without, therefore, human limiting characteristics such as memory failure and restrictions of any kind such as rights would imply. HOLY MEANS WHOLLY SEPARATE.

Yes, we may be forgetting God, but God will never "forget" us!

–March 2014

WHAT HAPPENED TO THE ANCIENT ONES?

We have retired them to the park bench outside the court house. No longer are they called to be expert witnesses. The park bench is where they can talk to each other. Whom do we call upon now to shape our verdicts? The young who are our peers. The up and coming. Not the out-going.

Recently in an adult study discussion at church, the question about the seniors in our society arose. *What is the reason that nowadays we no longer look to the older generation for wisdom and guidance, but seem to follow the young generation instead?* No one in the discussion had any answer for this question. But it made me begin to muse over this subject.

Why is it that youth in our culture have taken the place of seniors as trend setters and as the repository of knowledge and know-how? A number of possible factors have emerged in my mind since the question came up a couple of weeks ago. I am not sure of any of these, but together they may point to an answer.

(1) A shift in education of children from the old model of a teacher imparting truth to the young, to an approach which seeks to empower and enable children to discover truth for themselves.
(2) The urbanization of our society has removed children in the family from a position of necessary workers in the economic functioning of the family unit to a position of leisure and

as recipients of the free goods ands services produced by the parents.

(3) Technological developments so often seem to be adopted more easily by the young ahead of the understanding and acceptance of their parents.

(4) A change in family organization from a patriarchal type to an equalitarian arrangement in which father, mother and children tend to relate as equals.

(5) Economic opportunities for young people to earn significant funds, enabling them to do things on their own and putting them in a position to become objects of marketing advertising.

(6) Cultural challenging of individual and institutional authority of any kind.

This is not the whole story, I'm sure, but for me it is a start in understanding the current scene in which youth seem to have emerged in varying degrees as the new leaders of the society.

–March 2014

WHERE IS THE DIVINE?

It seems to me that there s a natural and universal inclination in each of us to elevate something to the level of divine. We have, I think, a normal need to worship some deity. Who, what or where is the deity in one's life is a most, if not the most, important question for each of us.

The range of possible answers to this question is limited to one's own self, some other human being(s), something(s) produced by humans, something(s) in the natural world, or nature itself, or God apart from this world, however one tries to describe God.

–March 2014

PLAQUE CHOKES

There is general agreement that *love*, however we try to define it, is a fundamental necessity in human life. A baby deprived of love will, if it survives, be scarred for life. We are born with the capacity and desire to reach out to others with what we call love. Some might say that the source of this "love and be loved" trait is our innate survival mechanism. Like the pet cat which rubs on your leg and wants to be petted. Or the family dog which shows you that it wants to be scratched under its chin.

However, poets sense that there is more to it than that sort of two dimensional definition of love. (Also those who have experienced love.) So, where does love come from? From what dimension does love emanate throughout our lives?

One of the most basic and far reaching descriptions of God in the Bible, I think, is that "God is love." I interpret this declaration to mean that God is the source of love. It is the love which comes from God into my life which is the love I must seek to offer to others. But much as I want to, there seems always some impediment, some obstruction in me which lessens or distorts love. I want to be a channel of God's love to others, but something in me gets in the way of a clear channel for loving others.

In musing over this problem, a metaphor comes to mind. It is the way in which we have discovered that the buildup of plaque in the human blood stream inhibits and eventually blocks the blood flow to the heart. As the heart is the source from which life-giving blood flows to all parts of the body through blood vessels, so God is the source from which love flows through us to others. As plaque in blood vessels chokes the flow of blood beyond the heart, so one's own self-centered "hang-ups" inhibit the full flow of love through us to others

My own self -concern, which is called "sin" in the Christian tradition, chokes off to varying extents the flow of God's love through me to others, as plaque in blood vessels chokes the flow of blood in our bodies.

–August 2014

THE PREVAILING WINDS OF FEAR

Having recently visited the HEART MOUNTAIN RELOCATION CAMP near Powell Wyoming, I became aware of the widespread fear in the U.S. of people of Japanese descent living in the United States during World War II. So fearful of the Japanese in our society were we that two months after Japan's attack on Pearl Harbor, an executive order was signed by President Franklin Roosevelt which would force tens of thousands of Japanese residents on the West Coast to be sent to relocation camps for the duration of the war. Stripped of their freedom, possessions and land, many were U.S. citizens. These neighbors of ours were forced into hastily built concentration camps inland from the coast, in which they would face extremely harsh conditions while they were surrounded by barbed wires fences and encircled by military guards over the next four years.

Fear of "Japs" was rampant, and many Americans felt sure that among these Japanese people were spies as well as agents of Japan who would do us harm. This national fear precipitated inhumane, unreasonable and un-American treatment of thousands of our harmless and productive neighbors. The prevailing winds of fear had blown us off course again.

Not many years earlier we feared the German-Americans among us during World War I. In compliance with this widespread attitude of fear, my grandfather, a pastor of a German Evangelical Church in

St. Louis, to refrain from conducting services in German as he had previously done with some regularity.

At he close of World War II, our national culture of fear focused upon Communism and the Communists whom we unreasonably suspected to be in our midst as undercover agents of the Soviet Union. This fear sullied the reputations of many loyal Americans and in some cases ruined their careers.

Such fear and accompanying hysteria always seem to destroy our capacity to respond reasonably to disturbing situations and to cause us to unjustly treat people whom we fear.

The winds of fear are sweeping us off our feet again. This time, after 9-11, our fears are focused upon followers of Islam in our midst and across the world whom we are quick to conclude may well be terrorists bent upon disrupting our way of life. Recently our fears have intensified in the wake of the grizzly beheading of an American journalist by Islamic extremists known as ISIS. Once again the prevailing winds of fear are putting us in danger of reacting unreasonably and losing sight of American values of freedom and justice.

–October 25, 2014

EIGHTY-SEVEN

Today I turn 87. It is my birthday. My father died when he was 87. That gives me pause. At the time he was in a nursing home confined to a wheel chair and was a victim of some form of dementia, probably Alzheimers Disease. Not having those conditions gives me a bit of confidence that 87 may very well not be my year of demise. A few months ago I consulted my new physician, after the retirement of my long time doctor. I can't even remember what complaint brought me to this consultation. Apparently something quite minor. Upon entering the room he looked at my chart and having presumably looked at my age said "You are doing quite well." Except for balance issues and loss of muscle strength, I also think I am doing quite well. My father's brother, Harvey, made it to 102. That gives me hope. But then again we live less than a hundred miles from the volatile caldera underneath Yellowstone Park from which increased rumblings have recently been detected. And when it blows, Bozeman is well within the radius in which total fatal destruction is predicted. So, it's 87 and counting–I guess.

"BLOOD BROTHERS"

Had I seen the book, *Blood Brothers,* on the shelf in a bookstore or on a listing on my Kindle, I doubt if I would have bought it. I don't usually read autobiographies, and books dealing with the Israeli-Palestine issue always seem to me to be too discouraging to hold much interest for me. However for my birthday my daughter Rose and family sent me an autobiography set amid the Israeli-Palestinian conflict. *Blood Brothers* is an autobiography by Elias Chacour and it deals with the history and current Israeli-Palestinian question with which Chacour's entire life has been concerned. I found it to be extremely inspiring, quite captivating, and very important. This is a significant account of a lifetime of effort to bring peaceful relationships between Jews and Palestinians, both Moslem and Christian, living in the same land–the Holy Land.

In sharing his life story of work toward reconciliation, Chacour shares his discoveries and understanding of the international maneuvering which forced the removal of Palestinians from their ancestral lands and sponsored the emigration of Jewish families into Palestine and of the violent chaos which followed and still persists today.

Elias Chacour grew up in a deeply Christian family in a small village by the Sea of Galilee. He tells of the Zionist take-over of his village and of the displacement of Palestinian families including his own. And he mourns the total destruction of his village.

He then testifies of how he feels God shaped his consciousness and called him to a ministry of reconciliation in the midst of the chaos of his times. Throughout his life he maintained his Christian conviction that Jews and Palestinians, both Christians and Moslems are blood brothers who are sons and daughters of Abraham, and that they should and can live together in peaceful harmony. To that end Elias Chacour has worked tirelessly.

Blood Brothers inspires the reader with the story of Chacour's peacemaking over the years in a most difficult region of the world, helps the reader to re-think the origins of this tragic situation, and challenges the reader to take part in peacemaking activities in whatever way he or she can.

"BUT I SAY UNTO YOU. . . ."

A recent commentary in *The Lewiston Tribune* by Marty Peterson, entitled "Troubled by Israel's Golden Rule," caught my eye and started me thinking. Peterson describes Israel's part in the cycle of violence against the Palestinians as a perverted Golden Rule: "Do unto others as others have done unto you." *Kill as many of theirs as they kill of ours.* The latest example is Israel's destruction of houses of innocent Palestinians in revenge for a killing of Jews by Palestinians recently.

And then I thought of the American right-wing satisfaction with this vicious cycle. There is, I think, a tragic coalition of the Zionist movement in Israel and conservative Christian misreading of Biblical prophecy. According to this confusion of thought, the second coming of Christ is seen by many conservative American Christians as dependent upon the restoration of the Jewish people to Jerusalem and the "Holy Land." Thus, according to this point of view, whatever Israel must do to attain this "divine right," is God's will regardless of the tragic fall-out for the Palestinians, many of whom by the way, are Christians. Add to this what seems to me to be undue Zionist sympathies motivating American right-wing politics uncritically to favor Israel's perverted "golden rule" of retribution.

Nearly 2000 years ago Jesus, in his Sermon on the Mount, addressed to his fellow Jews with a radical command to reverse their attitude and behavior. "You have heard that it was said, 'an eye for an eye and a tooth for a tooth . . .and you shall love your neighbor and hate your enemy,' but I say love your enemies and pray for those who persecute you." (Matthew 5: 38-39, 43-44)

This revolutionary new idea was given not only to the Jews of his time but to their descendants today and to his followers of every race and clan ever since.

How badly needed is this divinely commanded reversal from retribution to reconciliation in the Middle East and all across the world!

–December 2014

LEGACY? ARE THEY KIDDING?

In this season of Peace an advertisement came in our mail from a nearby congregation which was born out of anything but peace. It was from a church in Springhill calling itself "Springhill Presbyterian Church," which not so peacefully rejected its ties to the Presbyterian Church (U.S.A.) some months ago. One word misused in the advertisement has stimulated me to write a letter to that church session–a letter which I will not send, but if I did, it would be as follows:

To the Session of the X-Presbyterian Church of Springhill:

I am deeply offended by your use of the term, *legacy site* when referring to the facility on Walker Road because it was not in any sense bequeathed to you by the Presbytery of Yellowstone, as the term "legacy" would imply. You bought it from the Presbytery, which did not unanimously approve of this loss of its property for a very low price which should more truthfully be called a "steal." It is my opinion that the property on Walker Road to which you proudly refer is not an inheritance which you now enjoy, but stolen property which you are using. **Legacy–are you kidding?** –December 2014–Paul Krebill

–January 1, 2015

TRAGIC CONTRADICTIONS

New Year's Day brings us the annual countdowns of various news items–the ten best stories of last year. And other such notable events of the previous year. However I am struck by some tragic contradictions of the past year. Amid all the talk about whether or not we are safer now than in previous years, there are those who claim to be much safer because they carry concealed weapons to ward off any encroaching danger which may come their way. A young mother from Hayden, Idaho, apparently thought that way when she recently entered a WalMart store with a loaded pistol zipped into her hand bag. She placed her to year old toddler in her basket.

The child reached into her hand bag, found the gun and in picking it up fired it, killing his mother. A tragic contradiction to think that carrying a gun made her safer. An increasing number of states now allow concealed weapons and some allow guns to be carried by students in universities and other schools. I believe it is a tragic contradiction to believe that schools in those states are safer now than they were before the allowance of concealed weapons.

Another tragic contradiction can be found when one looks at the news coverage over the past year in our local newspaper. An alarming number of DUI's are handled by police in our area, many of which have resulted in devastating accidents. The percentage of highway deaths in which alcohol was a factor is shameful. Reports of alcohol-related domestic violence as well as public disturbances in various Main Street gatherings are often published in our paper. And reports of rape and other acts of violence and mayhem on our university campus also frequently cite alcohol consumption as a contributing factor.

All this, while at the same time one reads about a surprising increase in the number of new breweries which have begun to dot the landscape of the Bozeman business community. On December 26 the newspaper reported the opening of a new brewery and tasting room in Bozeman very near to Interstate 90 which the owner is hoping will create a sense of community on this side of town." Rather, I believe there is a tragic contradiction when we as a town offer more and more breweries and distilleries while at the same time devastation due to alcohol use seems to be increasing as well.

Yet another tragic contradiction is to be seen when one compares the front page article of the December 26 paper under the headline: "*Serving Bozeman–Community Café open seven days a week including Christmas,*" with the price of some of the real estate in the area. This "pay what you can" café and also Bozeman's homeless shelter are God-sends to our many neighbors who do not have enough to eat, some of whom are homeless as well. Such lack of basic necessities is tragically in contradiction to homes selling at more than a million dollars.

A happier New Year will come if we have more ample measures of prudence, wisdom and justice among us in 2015.

–February 2015

NOBODY'S GOING TO TELL US WHAT TO DO

Disturbing and saddening are the reports of Presbyterian congregations opting to leave the denomination ostensibly because the General Assembly is allowing Presbyterian clergy to perform marriages of same sex couples in states in which that is permitted. When challenged, some of these folk go on to claim that what they really don't agree with is a denomination which doesn't "follow the Bible." Somehow this is supposed to give a more credible basis for the extreme action of leaving the very denomination which had nurtured them. But I think this reference to the use of the Bible is also an excuse to cover up what I really think is going on.

I think there is a deeply entrenched anti-authority mood in many congregations. Down deep there is a feeling in members of congregations and many times in their pastors as well, which can be expressed in the declaration–felt but never said– "Nobody's going to tell us what to do."

I believe this strong anti-authoritarian stance on the part of congregations and clergy is an extension of this same mood which prevails in our American culture today. An example of this point of view is the Tea Party movement in politics, and also the Libertarian Party point of view, both of which resist taxation and regulations by government entities.

I suspect that if one were to poll the congregations and pastors leaving our denomination today, one would find that the majority would be on the political right with Tea Party and Libertarian tendencies to varying extents! "Nobody's going to tell us what to do."

There is room in our Presbyterian Church for varying convictions on the matter of gay marriage, and there are substantial variations in our denomination of how one is to read and interpret the Bible. But it is those who are infected with the American deification of unrestrained personal freedom who don't seem to find it in their hearts to submit to the will and the wisdom of the church of which they have been a member. "Nobody is going to tell us what to do."

–February 2015

THE "CHRISTIAN MARRIAGE" MUDDLE

For whom may we perform Christian marriage? This has been a muddle for Presbyterian clergy over the years. At the time of my ordination in 1952, the issue centered around divorce. We were allowed to marry divorced persons in only certain circumstances which had to do the with the reasons for the particular divorce in the case of those seeking marriage. As I remember we were not ordinarily to marry divorced persons. Over time the restrictions were gradually lifted. At one stage in this loosening of restrictions upon Presbyterian clergy, we were to present a proposed marriage case in question to our presbytery to seek permission to perform such a marriage. Subsequently the matter was left to the discretion of the clergyperson.

Later in my time of ministry it became common practice to perform the marriage of any and all whom seek to be married by a Christian clergy person using a Christian marriage service. In the majority of these cases in my experience the ceremony took place in the church building. In fact, in my earliest years I required this. At that time it was the tacit assumption that such folk were Christian at least in the broadest sense of the word. Church membership was not an issue.

As far as I know it was rare in those days for a couple seeking marriage to be turned down. In my years of ministry, I turned down only one such couple. The woman asked me not to mention God or to offer any prayers in the service. I told her the only service I could provide would be a Christian service which of course would include reference and prayer to God. As I reflect upon this difficult impasse, I see now that she and I both were being honest, with her atheist position and my Christian conviction at odds.

Now, decades later, those without Christian faith, if they are honest would not ask a Christianclergy person to perform their marriage. I suspect that sea captains and justices of the peace have had in increase in business lately. The majority, it would seem, look around for the nicest church building and try to schedule a wedding there. Then in most cases this will involve engaging the resident clergy to perform the service if he or she is willing to accommodate. These churches and pastors may or may not be willing to provide these services.

A couple may arrange for the church building, but discover that the pastor will not help them. Then the couple must find the police chaplain or some other clergy, possibly a retired clergy uncle from another state. For a lot of folk, I think it is much like finding a photographer A much more prevalent arrangement these days is for the couple to find a unique place to be married, perhaps a commercial marriage venue of some kind, and then to find a clergyperson to come and perform the marriage. If neither of the folk wanting to be married has a church connection, finding an officiant may be a problem. Commercial wedding chapels in Nevada are an extreme example of this secularization of marriage.

Christian marriage is a muddle. The focus of the muddle has been on the word and meaning of *Christian*. In this changing social pattern there is, I think, an increasing number of Christian clergy who perform only weddings which are by definition Christian, to couples in which at least one is a confessing Christian and who desires Christian marriage. The muddle is clearing up a bit as Christians have Christian marriages and others have civil marriages without the trappings of religion. Thus, the word *Christian* is becoming more authentic.

Now the muddle is in facing the issue of same sex marriage. This is another aspect of the gay-lesbian controversy which has been threatening the peace and unity of the Presbyterian Church for years. Now the heated question before the church concerns whether or not Presbyterian clergy should be permitted to perform such marriages.

Once again Presbyterians are lined up against one another because of deep disagreement over how homosexuality should be seen–whether or not is willful, whether or not it is sinful, and how the Bible in this matter is to be understood.

The question now has to do with the definition of *marriage,* not how one should understand homosexuality.. I believe society needs a new term for the legal union of people of the same gender. The definition of *marriage* has traditionally been the legal binding of a man and woman to become, husband and wife. Thus, the term *same sex marriage* requires a radical redefinition of the term *marriage.* Therein lies the muddle. Commonly understood, marriage has referred to a covenant between a woman and a man. It is a legal union in which, I believe, society has a stake for the orderly succession of generations.

Those of us for whom marriage is the sacred covenant union of a man and a woman find it very difficult, if not impossible, to dilute the term, *marriage*, to include homosexual relationships.

A departure from this union between genders, I think requires another term for same sex unions. It is probably too late at this juncture to institute in our society an alternative term for same sex unions. Had we found such a term, I think much of the controversy might not have developed in our church., and perhaps not in the broader society as well. But with one term to fit all the muddle continues.

55 YEAR RETURN

After our son, Ross, died in January of 1960, Doris and I "adopted" a little boy in the Palmer Children's home in Columbus, Mississippi, meaning that we sent financial contributions to the Presbyterian sponsored orphanage in the name of this particular boy, and the home would send us information about him. We lived in Bozeman at the time, where I was a campus pastor at Montana State University. We continued our relationship to the little boy in the orphanage for two years.

Now, fifty five years later, our second son, Dan, who was one year old when Ross died, is at Palmer Home in Mississippi this week with a group of MSU university students for whom he is pastor, on a mission trip. The Bozeman group is doing volunteer work at the Palmer Home and spending time with the children.

A poignant return for our family, fifty-five years later.

—March 13, 2015

P.S. Dan checked with the Palmer Home and did not find any record of a gift from us in 1960. Since our memory is a bit hazy, it may be that the children's home to which we contributed was another Presbyterian-related home in the deep South, perhaps in Alabama. In a less specific way, however, Dan's return was nevertheless significant for us as a family

–March 13, 2015

CHRISTMAS LETTERS

Doris is going over last year's Christmas letters and cards in preparation for her efforts along this line next December. She handed me three letters from close friends which gave me pause to think again of significant loss. One of the letters was from a son of Herb Strom written a few months after Herb's death in September of 2014. The other was from Lad Anderson, written a month before his death in August of 2014. Gerard Kuiper, still another close friend, died in 2014.

And then I thought of three other close friends of many years, of Joe Degi who also died in 2014, of John Jones who died in 2006, and of Jack Wells whose death also was in 2006.

As I ponder my life time, I conclude that there remain only three whom I would name as close friends over the years: Ricky Gill from my childhood in Oak Park, with whom I still have contact; And John Schroeder and George Langeler from those very good days at Elmhurst, whose friendships continue. And so, I look forward to their Christmas letters for this year.

–April 2015

AGAINST THE LAW

In today's news both Indiana and Arkansas are in controversy over legislation proposed in each of these states to allow people and businesses to deny services which would violate their own religious convictions. Proponents affirm that religious freedom should allow such religious based denials of services. Those opposed claim that this legislation is an attempt to allow businesses to discriminate against gays and lesbians. Their position would in effect make it against the law for a Christian to hold to his or her religious principles in cases in which the Christian is asked to provide services which go against his or her convictions.

It seems to me this is a *Christian vs. Culture* issue which poses three options to the Christian. (1) Change the culture-- change the law as in the case of the proposed legislation; (2) Go against your own convictions–abide by the law as opponents of the legislation ask of the Christian; (3) Stand up for your convictions–break the law and suffer the consequences.

In the earliest centuries when Christians lived under Rome and its emperor, many Christians chose the third option(Option 3) when they were required to worship the Caesar, they refused and they paid the price of their sacrifice for Christ–persecution and sometimes death. After centuries in the Western world in which the culture had changed to suit Christians, (Option1) many of us have gotten so accustomed to living in a "Christian culture" that we have gone along with whatever the culture dictates.(Option 2)

But now, as our culture has pushed religious faith more and more to the sidelines and has become secularized, could it be that Christians are called upon to stand up for their convictions which may be quite contrary to those of the culture? (Option 3)–even though that puts us against the law with whatever consequences that might incur? I wonder.

PART 3

TINYBUBBLES

Here are some tiny bubbles of insight or observation:

Lonely in the digital age... Being a child in the digital age is eating the hamburger your father bought you in McDonalds while he visits with someone else on his cell phone

Envy excludes interest. Those who are envious of something I have done, are not apt to express any interest in knowing about my accomplishment.

The "shelf" looks good. . . for someone else. When I was in my late 30s, during discussions here in Bozeman about what sort of retirement facility should be developed, one of the consultants commented that younger adults were quite interested in developing retirement facilities, while seniors ready to retire were reluctant to think much about such projects. At the time this difference in interest seemed strange to me. One would have thought that the closer one is to retirement the more interested one would be in planning such facilities. Not so, and now I know why! It is with great reluctance that one wants to be "put on the shelf," so to speak.

If I don't own it, I won't cut it. Quite a number of homes in Bozeman are situated on the edge of their neighborhood so that their back yards face a busy street passing by their location. In many cases the view of their house and yard is spoiled by a border of out-of-control grass and weeds growing on the right-of-way for the arterial street. I suspect the view is spoiled by an attitude for the home owner which goes something like this: "I won't cut it, if I don't own it."

Sun or a Moon? Which are you? How does the mood of another person affect you? When a person comes into the room with a sullen attitude do you find yourself feeling sullen or sad as well? Or doesn't that affect you? If you feel sunny, do you stay sunny no matter what the other person appears to feel like? I think some of us are like the moon which reflects however much light comes to it, while others of us are like the sun which generates its own light. So be it. I'm not sure you can change which heavenly body you resemble.

Despite their favorite rationalization guns kill people, the N.R.A. not withstanding.

Arrogance is the opposite of faith. I have often sensed that those who refuse to accept in faith that Jesus is God in human flesh, tend to be quite proud of the fact, and sometimes look with disdain on those of us so blind as to have faith in Christ who in some sense is the Son of God. In place of the humility of ***faith*** is the arrogance of placing onself on a par with Jesus.

A curious 180 degree switch-around is becoming evident these days. Just when *marriage* seems to be replaced with the less binding term--*relationship* for many heterosexual arrangements, many homosexual couples want *marriage* instead of *relationship* to describe their arrangement

Might we be experiencing a 180 degree switch-around in the definitions we use for heterosexual and homosexual; arrangements as to who will be married in the future and who will be in relationships?

After all some words do change in their definitions over the centuries, even to meanings which are opposites to the original definitions.

Now, what do you think of that?

Ashamed of being a man? Women with strong feminist conviction frequently speak in such a way that makes me come away ashamed of being a man. This happened to me again last night when I attended a lecture at the university which focused on the women who entered the Park Service in the early days of Yellowstone National Park, facing a strong male-dominated organization. It was as if the underlying mood of the speaker and many of her listeners was one of the victory of good over evil. And so when asked what percentage of park rangers today are women, it was with great satisfaction that the listeners heard the speaker say that she was pretty sure that there are now more women rangers in the National Park Service than men--- and I came away feeling like one of the evil ones, were losing the battle.

"Too Tottery" A long time ago when I was pastor of the Presbyterian Community Church of Yoder, Wyoming, I asked an elderly member if he would take part in a worship service which I was planning. His immediate answer shocked me and I have remembered that exchange ever since that day. His reply was: "I can't. I'm too tottery." At the time my age was twenty-seven. I did not understand the elderly church member's reluctance because he was "too tottery." Sixty years later I am now eighty-seven and I have recently turned a young man down, who asked me to judge a debate at his high school. Though I did not explain at the time, my turn-down was because I am too tottery.

LinkedOUT??? Sometime ago I unknowingly got myself on ***LINKEDIN***. I don't want to be on this (or any other) social network. I cannot find out how to get disconnected. There is no such thing as a telephone to tell someone to write me off. Their "HELP" options give you all sorts of things you can do **except get off.** Apparently once on **LINKEDIN,** you're on for life–and then some. The latest listing of people who want to be linked to me included a friend of mine who passed away a number of years ago. So, I guess, once linkedin you're linked in for **ETERNITY.** Quite remarkable, I'd say.

P.S. Unless, of course, you can find a granddaughter who can unlink you!

PART 4

CONCLUSION

Life is like an URN freshly turned on the POTTER'S WHEEL, empty and waiting to be filled: first with depending on the POTTER'S loving. . . . then with life-long acting and experiencing. . . . and finally, when one's URN is almost full, it is blessed with remembering.

So to close my musing I include this simple German Children's song.
IN DER STILLEN EINSAMKEIT.

A 17th century hymn was sung in German by Amish school children to the tune "Jesus Loves Me" at the beginning of each school day. According to Donald Kraybill in Amish Grace, this was sung on the morning of the schoolhouse shooting rampage in Nickel Mines, Pennsylvania in October of 2006 (Kraybill, Nolt, Weaver-Zercher, AMISH GRACE, Josey-Bass, Sanfrancisco, p 21)

In der Stillen Einsamkeit, Findest du mein lob bereitGrosser Gott Erhöre mich, Denn mein Herze suche dich. Unveränderlich bisht du, nimmer shtill und doch in ruhYahreszeiten du regiersht, und sie ordenlich einführsht. Diese kalte winder luft, mit enfindung gräft ruftSehet welch ein starker Herr, Summer Winder macheter.

IN QUIET SOLITUDE

In quiet solitude,
You will find your praise prepared,
Great God, hear me,
For my heart seeks you.
You are unchanging,
Never still and yet at rest.
You rule the seasons of the year,
And bring them in at proper time.

BOOK II

AUTOBIOGRAPHICAL FACTS, IMPRESSIONS AND MEMORIES

INTRODUCTION

A time to be born and a time to die
A time to plant and a time to pluck up
A time to weep and a time to laugh
A time to keep and a time to throw away
Ecclesiastes 3

As I think about this second Book of *AUTUMN REFLECTIONS* which is to be made up of my own life stories– I wonder how one records 90 plus years of living? I have chosen to offer my story as it unfolded in the various places I have lived by way of present-day memories and feelings which those places engender in me.

But there is more to life memories than that of places. What about the persons who entered into my story in each place? And what about plotting life's course? What did we do? What happened over those past years now long gone? Who were the persons who helped to shape my life in those times and places?

It strikes me that, as in a novel, there are settings, characterizations and plot to be seen in one's own life story.

The past exists through its imprints on our lives in the present, through memories, often enhanced through memorabilia of one kind or another, and through the relationships with others in various places and times which remain.

I have recently received a long letter from Dorothy Hicks addressed to Doris and me. She was Dorothy Martin, a young teenager in our youth group in the Yoder Church (1952-1956). We also get extensive letters from another girl in our Wyoming youth group, whom we knew as Berta Kay Likins. She is now Alberta Haas and for a time she and her husband were members of St. Andrew Church in Billings. These two friends are examples of persons from past places who are still very much a part of our lives even though the places in which we encountered them have long since receded into the quiet past. Similarly, folks who were church members in the Oreti Parish in New Zealand have become regular correspondents. When the earthquake struck Christchurch, we e-mailed some of them with family in Christchurch to check on their well-being.

Plot, or story line, as well as places and persons also has a continuing influence. Had we not developed a youth group in Yoder or gone to New Zealand to serve as the pastor of a parish there, these continuing personal relationships would not have come about.

And so, even though my story is organized around the places I have lived, be assured that there's more to it than that: namely persons and plot! Those elements will also be memorialized in the following pages.

PART 1

PRE-HISTORY

However let me introduce our story with some *Pre-history* which could be called: FOUR ROOT STREAMS CONVERGING. With the marriage of Paul Krebill and Doris Schoening on August 19, 1950, our four grandparents' life stories converged to become our story.

Paul's roots In 1819 in the town of Schorndorf, a few miles east of Stuttgart, Germany, my **maternal** great great grandfather, Jacob J. Knauss, was born into a family who were members of the newly formed Evangelical Prussian Union Church with roots in both the Reformed and the Lutheran churches in Germany.

At the same time, about 100 miles to the west, my **paternal** great great grandfather, Friedrich Krebill, owned and operated a farm, called Messerschwanderhof, near Otterberg in the Rhineland-Pfalz region of Germany. Eight years after Jacob Knauss's birth at Schorndorf in 1827, Peter Krebill was born, the seventh child of Friedrich and Anna Krebill. (His birth was eight years after Jacob Knauss's birth at Schorndorf) The Krebill family members were devout Mennonites. When Peter was six years old in 1833, he and his family left Germany and sailed to America, where Friedrich bought a farm near Hayesville, Ohio.

A few years later Jacob Knauss also emigrated to America after having attended theological school at Basel. In 1842 Jacob Knauss was called to begin his ministry in the New World. He lived in Philadelphia for a winter before he was accepted by the Kirchenverein (the German Evangelical Church in North America) in 1844.

Jacob Knauss was then sent to Missouri to become the pastor of the Evangelical Church in Manchester. Jacob's daughter, Sophie, married Karl Braun. Their second child was Theodore Braun.

It happened that during Jacob's tenure at Manchester, Missouri, Peter Krebill moved to a town about 200 or so miles north of Manchester, in Lee County, Iowa. There he bought a farm at Franklin Center. He became a member of the local Mennonite congregation. His seventh child was Peter R. who, after his marriage to Ida Leize, moved to Donnelson in Lee County, Iowa, where he owned a grain mill.

In 1898 Peter R. Krebill and his wife, Ida, gave birth to a son, Armin Peter. When Armin was a small child the family moved a few miles into Ft. Madison, where they became members of St. John's Evangelical Church.

By the early 1920s Armin Krebill attended Eden Seminary in the St. Louis area, having graduated from Elmhurst College in Illinois, a "Pro-seminar" of the Evangelical Church.

By this time, Theodore Braun, a grandson of Jacob J. Knauss, was pastor to St. James Evangelical Church in St. Louis. It was the custom of Rev. Braun, and his wife, Louise, to invite Eden Seminary students to their home for Sunday dinner. It was during these occasions that Armin Krebill met and fell in love with Theodore Braun's daughter, Louise.

And so it was that in 1926 Friedrich Krebill's great grandson, Armin Krebill, and Jacob Knauss's great grand daughter, Louise Braun, were married in the parsonage of St. James Evangelical Church in St. Louis.

Thus, this was a providential convergence of the Krebill journey from the Rhineland Pfalz region of Germany and of the Knauss journey from the province of Wurtemberg, Germany. Each family crossed the Atlantic and moved westward to the American Midwest.

In a little over a hundred year, descendants of Friedrich Krebill and Jacob Knauss were joined in marriage.

In this way, as a child of that marriage, I share equally in the German Mennonite heritage of Friedrich Krebill of Otterberg, Germany and the German Evangelical heritage of Jacob J. Knauss of Schorndorf, Germany.

(I am indebted to Olga Krebill Hirschler for information regarding the Krebill family history and to my good friend, John Schroeder, whose research has brought to light information about the Knauss and Braun family histories.)

Doris roots: Carl Friederick Heinrich (Schoening) Hopfner was born on December 23, 1864 at Alt Klieth, in the Church Parish at Mollin in Gros Herzogthum (Dukedom) of Mecklenburg Schwerin. His mother died when he was an infant and his grandmother raised him. He took her name of Schoening. He was a goose herder and as a small boy was struck by lightning. His companion was killed in this episode. Carl was saved by his little dog which pulled his head up out of the puddle of water in which his face was immersed during the storm. However, this accident resulted in deafness in one ear for the rest of his life. When he turned sixteen his grandmother brought him to America so that he would not have to serve in the army. Carl was small in stature, only 5' 1" and never weighed more than 140 pounds.

Wilhelmine, Sophia, Friederike Reissener was born on April 9th in 1869 at Trollhagen in the Dukedom Mecklenbkurg Strelitz.. Her mother was Johanna Reissner. She emigrated to the U.S. with her husband and three children, one of whom, a son, died aboard ship on the passage across the Atlantic. Wilhelmina and another brother with their parents settled in LaSalle, Illinois. Later on the brother moved to Nebraska where he farmed

Caroline Hoeft was born in 1857 at Wonzow Kreis Flatou, in West Preusen. She married Julius Joop. In later years Caroline described her experiences in Germany, speaking of thatched roofed houses without wooden floors, and torches for lamps. Her father had been a shepherd, having three hired men and a hired girl. Besides the house, she remembers a shed used for slaughtering, and for smoking. It was where the hired men and the dogs slept. She said that they did their own spinning and weaving, making their own clothes and that they wore wooden shoes. Their principal foods were potatoes, soup, herring, bacon and oatmeal. Their health had been good.

Julius and Caroline (Hoeft) Joop emigrated to North America and settled in LaSalle, Illinois In telling of this passage in later years Caroline said that they traveled third class, carrying bedding and baskets with them. Boards were used for beds. They got seasick during the voyage and finally landed on Ellis Island. At first the couple live with Caroline's sister. Four years later Caroline becomes quite homesick for Germany and returns, staying a year and three months. However, she does not like Germany as well as her new home in Illinois, feeling that there is more money and more freedom in America. She retained a desire to visit Germany.

On January 28,th 1890 Julius Joop and his wife, Carolina (Hoeft) Joop gave birth to Louise Wilhelmina. She was the fourth of seven children. Two other girls: Marie and Caroline, and four boys: William, Julius, Rudolph, and Carl.

As a young man, Carl (Charles) Schoening emigrated to North America. He came to LaSalle, Illinois where he went to work for the Mattheson-Hegler Zinc Company. On August 6th of 1888 Carl Schoening married Wilhellmine Reissener in LaSalle Illinois. He became foreman of the pottery, a post he would hold for twenty-six years, after which he worked as a watchman at the plant. He bought a home at 720 Ninth Street in which he and his wife, Wilhellmine raised their family.

Their first child, Wilhelm, Friederich, Gustav, later known as William, was born on the 22nd of May in 1890 at 9 PM (Thursday) Eight more children were born, three boys: Herman, Carl who died before his second birthday, and Albert, and five daughters: Hertha who lived not quite one year, Louise, Emma, Hildegard, and Elsie, who died a few days after her birth.

William Schoening and Louise Joop married on November 25,th 1914 in the German Lutheran Church of LaSalle. (Now Trinity United Church of Christ) After high school William took a course at Browns Business School in LaSalle, and then began work as office boy in the Mattheson-Hegler Zinc Company in LaSalle. By the time of his retirement many years later he had become treasurer of the company. He and his wife bought a home at 860 O'Connor Avenue in which they lived for the rest of their lives, except for a short time when Louise was in a nursing home before her death on February 18, 1969.

William and Louise Schoening gave birth to four children, three boys and one girl: Karl, William. Doris, and Kurt, all of whom were educated in the public schools of LaSalle. After her high school graduation in 1943 Doris worked for the Westclox Company in Peru, Illinois. In the fall of 1945 she enrolled in Elmhurst College, Elmhurst, Illinois. Louise died on February 18. 1969, and William died four hours before his 86th birthday on May 21, 1976

My own memories *and impressions. . . .*

After reading Heirloom by David Mas Masomoto, which is made up of letters he writes to people in his family and circle of friends, through which he recounts memories of his childhood and later life as a peach farmer in the Central Valley of California, I have been inspired to do something similar His style and the simple content of his memories sets the pace for what follows, as a legacy to leave behind to my family and friends about what it was like to be Paul Krebill growing up in Chicago and Oak Park and then going out into the world from there.

A lot of people my age are doing this sort of thing for their children and grandchildren. Doris and others in our family have told me on a number of occasions that such a life story is something we ought to do.

And so I share the following.

Engrafting from my rootstocks. . . .

Apart from the passing on of genetic imprint from one generation to the next, I have become aware of what I would refer to as the engrafting of one generation from the rootstock of one's ancestors (Or at least in my case.) I have come to see that in large part my personality and consciousness are the result of my engrafting into the rootstock of my parents.

Most influential in the formation of the Krebill rootstock was its Mennonite tradition. Donald B. Kraybill, an expert on the Anabaptist expressions in American life (and a very distant relative) characterizes this tradition with the German word *gelassenheit* – submissiveness, which results in a personality which is reserved, modest, calm, and quiet. He shows that the Mennonite tradition values submission, obedience, humility, thrift, simplicity, and refuses any form of violence. Mennonites, generally speaking, separate themselves from the world, except for acts of service to the needs of others. They discourage attitudes or actions which put one's self forward. Furthermore, I believe that this set of personality traits separates one from the mainstream of American culture and avoids competitive behavior.

This characterization to a great extent describes my father, the rootstock onto which I was grafted. Now in later life I recognize these personality traits and attitudes in myself. To name a few examples of why I think this reveals something of my consciousness: I have always felt that down deep I don't belong in the mainstream of the culture around me; I detest arrogance in anyone; I find violence to any degree as repulsive; I have never been competitive. I am sure that there is more to be said, but at this point I do think that the Mennonite Krebill rootstock has played a significant part in who I am.

The Braun rootstock on my mother's side is more difficult to identify. But as I think about it now, I would point to the fact that my mother's family was heavily involved in the German Evangelical Church of North America. Many of her male forebears and contemporary family members were clergy: her father, her uncle, and her brother, well as two brothers-in-law. From within my mother's family I had a first cousin and two second cousins once removed who were Evangelical clergy. All of these men had their college-pre seminary education at Elmhurst College in Illinois. And so when I enrolled in Elmhurst college I entered the tradition of these relatives and was further engrafted into my maternal rootstock. My first cousin, Ted Braun, who became an Evangelical pastor, was a year; ahead of me at Elmhurst. When I entered Elmhurst, in one of his first conversations with me he announced that we had thirty-six relatives in the student body. On the walls of Elmhurst's Old

Main I found in the assortment of class pictures of both my grandfather and my father.

In reflecting on my German Evangelical heritage, I am aware of its progressive social involvement. At risk of sounding like a name dropper, I note that the Niebuhr family came out of this theological and social tradition. My grandfather had been a fellow pastor with Gustav Niebuhr, father of his well-known sons, in the Evangelical church in Missouri and Illinois and my uncle served as an assistant pastor to Reinhold Niebuhr in an Evangelical church in Detroit. H. Richard Niebuhr at one time served as president of Elmhurst College.

Interestingly enough the Mennonite root and the Evangelical root became intertwined in my own father's life. At an early age his family left a Mennonite Church to join a German Evangelical church. Subsequently my father entered Elmhurst and joined its procession of pre-seminary students. He subsequently married Louise Braun. He went on to Eden Seminary for two years before deciding to become a teacher instead of a pastor.

As these two traditions intertwined, I wonder what this meant for my father as his own Mennonite position of separation from the world met the Evangelical passion for social justice. For me this has resulted in my believing in social justice causes but being unwilling to march in promotion of peace and justice issues.

PART 2

GLIMPSES FROM CHILDHOOD

Chester, Illinois Though I was born in Deaconess Hospital in St. Louis, Missouri, at the time of my birth and for about a year following, my parents lived in Chester, Illinois where my father taught in the local high school. Chester is on the Mississippi River about sixty miles southeast of St. Louis. My parents rented an apartment in the home of Dr. And Mrs. James. He was a general practitioner. I, of course, have no memories of this period in my life, but some years later when I was a small child, I remember visiting the James's, with whom we must have had a close relationship. I remember sitting on the front porch with my father and Dr. James before going into the dining room for lunch. I was enthralled with Dr. James's explanation of why he had three cars, an unbelievable number of vehicles for one man to own in those days. One, he said was for his house calls, a shiny black coupe, a second for use as a family car, and the third for muddy days, an older dirty sedan.

Years later, when Mac Stevens, a member of St. Andrew Church in Billings gave me a Chevy pick-up his engineering firm no longer needed, I thought of Dr. James and his three cars. Now I would have two vehicles or the next thirty-five years.

We sat at a round dining room table. I was seated next to Dr. James who instructed me on how to use the little glass salt cellar at my place. I was advised to dip my radish in the salt to make it taste better.

Chicago, Illinois When I was nearly two years old we moved to Chicago in the Austin neighborhood. My father took a job teaching math and physics at Austin High School where he would remain until he retired as head of the Math department, many years later.

Columbus Park–Chicago, Illinois. This was not far from where we lived in the Austin neighborhood on the west edge of the city. I have fond memories of walking in Columbus Park with my parents when I was four or five years old. The little foot paths intrigued me then and ever since. Even today I like to walk the travel paths in nearby park areas. I remember one particular place along the path which I especially enjoyed. The path divided for a few feet with half of it mounting a slight rise and going forward while the other half of the path went along side of the mound on a lower level. With great glee I would walk the upper path and while my parents took the lower one. This always brought my father to repeat the phrase from the Scottish song: "I'll take the high road, and ye'll take the low road." There was a lake and some sort of boat house with wooden rowboats. I don't remember ever having been in one of the boats.

Monroe Street at Central Avenue in Chicago I think the address of our apartment building was 5568 Monroe. There were probably three or four entrances into four apartments in a two story building. It might have been three stories. It was a fairly large building built up to the sidewalk extending eastward from Central Avenue. Ours was a first floor apartment at the west end of the complex. Beyond our building to the east were separate two story houses down the rest of the block. The Dannon family lived in the apartment above us. They were Jewish. They had a daughter, Joyce. I remember her vividly but I do not remember playing with her. I really don't remember playmates as such in this neighborhood. The Dienharts lived in the house just east of us. We knew them. Their family was made up of a divorced mother, a couple of children and maybe a grandmother, I'm not sure. I have a slight memory of the boy, who was about my age. I remember taking walks with my mother east down the block and around the corner. The side street had an apartment building with basement windows at the edge of the sidewalk. "Mr. Johnson," my imaginary friend, lived behind one of the those windows.

Madison Street was a block north of Monroe. This was a major commercial street stretching west from the "Loop" downtown. The "Loop" referred to the rectangular loop around which all of the elevated trains went. Under the elevated tracks were the main business streets of downtown. Marshall Field's was the most well known of the stores in the Loop. At the intersection of Madison and Central was Emmet School, the grade school in which my formal education began with Kindergarten. In order to get there from our apartment, we had to cross Madison. My Mother always took me to school and met me after school. In my memory, Emmet school was big, and very dark, both in its woodwork and interior colors and in its lighting. For this reason and because I was very shy, Emmet school was very forbidding. The only memory of Kindergarten I have was of one day when I was given the opportunity to take my turn to go to the big toy box and pick out the toy we would play with that day. I picked out a ball. This, however, as it turned out, did not indicate athletic interest or ability. While I remained in Emmet School for first and the early part of second grade, I have only vague diffuse memories of those months.

Already before I began school, it was the daily pattern in our three-member family to take a ride after my father returned home from Austin High School where he was a math teacher. He got home around three to three-thirty. These rides usually involved shopping stops here and there. My earliest memories of such shopping were at Madigans, a home furnishings store on Madison Street not too far to the east of Central, and at chain grocery stores, which were later named named Jewel. I'm not sure what they were called then–something like "Lubalows," I think. The prevailing exterior color of these stores was white and dark brown. Other grocery chains were the A & P which had a red logo and Krogers with a green decor. We never went to these. I have the impression my mother thought they were a cut below the Jewel stores. I used to like rides on the dark winter evenings. The neon lights especially attracted me, especially the royal to dark blue ones. One sign had movement and I remember it vividly. It was a rather large round neon sign over a small barbeque shop. The moving lights depicted a chicken over a fire being tended by a cook. Beneath the sign was a round glassed-in barbeque pit over which one could see chickens roasting

Cars were very important to my father. He took great delight in whatever car he had. His first car was a Model T Ford, two passenger coupe. I don't know the year, but I assume it must have been a 1925 or 1926 model. He had bought it new, the only new car he ever had. If I remember it, the only memory which comes to mind is a fleeting image of it with my father in or near it. I think it was black. This was during the depth of the Depression. I remember the afternoon my father came home telling us that the Model T had been stolen off the parking lot at school. I still see him standing in the doorway in his long overcoat with his hat still on looking forlorn, telling us that. From then on we had used cars. I don't know how long it was before we bought a Dodge Bros. blue coupe. I remember the little name plate on the top strip of the radiator which had the Dodge symbol. For some reason my mother liked the Dodge especially much. A few years later my father traded the Dodge in on a Studebaker. He was sold the top model, known as President. It was four door black, and to me seemed huge. The day after driving it home we took it for a longer drive–to Milwaukee, I think was our intention. But not far out it began to heat up and boil over. My father took it back to the dealer and exchanged it for a Studebaker Commander, a bit more modest. It was tan in color and I believe must have been about a 1931 model. I think we kept this for many years. I can still remember how those cars smelled when we first got them, usually a rich leather, slightly musty smell.

One Saturday we drove into Chicago to the Olson Rug factory, which had a special outdoor program. In an open space next to the building a simulated mountain cliff had been built with, I think, a waterfall flowing down the side into a pool of some sort. The program was to feature some Indians up on this cliff, I suppose dancing and drumming, I'm not sure, My mother was always cold, so as was our custom, she brought a blanket in which to view this program. Her favorite blanket had an Indian design in bright red, yellow, and blue. When we parked and got out of the car to walk to where there were chairs for a small audience, one of the Company officials greeted us and led us to the front row and gave us some special seats. I'm not sure when it dawned on my parents, but eventually they concluded that we were mistaken for some of the Indians.

My parents were members of First English Evangelical Church on Palmer Square in Chicago. They were close friends with Will Schuessler, the organist. The minister was Dr. Louis Goebel. This is where I first went to Sunday School, the first day of which terrified me. I was very shy. In fact our little family of three was pretty much the extent of my early social environment. Once in a while we would be invited to the Schuessler's for dinner and they would come to our home for dinner. I don't remember Will's wife's first name. Mr. Schuessler was an assistant principal at a Chicago high school somewhere. They had two children, both older than I. Lenore was the oldest. Norman was younger, perhaps four ore five years older than I. The most vivid in my memory were the visits at Christmas time to their home. They lived in a yellow brick bungalow in a part of Chicago north of Oak Park. Norman had an extensive electric train set up under the Christmas tree of which I was quite envious. Their Christmas tree was artificial and ornately decorated There was no one else with whom we exchanged visits.

Visits from relatives were infrequent. Once in a while my uncle Harvey would stay with us when he had a layover in Chicago. He was a railway postal clerk with routes mostly in central Illinois. I don't remember much about his visits. I remember taking my mother's uncle Jacob to the downtown train station, Union Station, in connection with his many trips as a home mission secretary for the Evangelical Church. He always referred to his suitcase as his "grip."

I can still hear the pulsing of the giant steam engines as they slowly backed into the station to deposit passengers from afar, coming into Chicago from cities to the east and the west. In the winter there might be snow clinging to the undercarriages, evidence that the train had gone through snow storms on its way into Chicago. Sometimes when we walked along the platform under an exterior roof we could see people in the dining car eating. All this, together with the hubbub in the terminal building was very exciting.

Another vivid memory from my child is that of the Auto Show. In those days it was held in the Stockyards Amphitheater on the south side. Each year my father would take me to the auto exposition in which automobile companies displayed their new models. Some years we were accompanied by my uncle Harvey. We would walk from one company's area to the next, looking at all the new models. Attendants would be constantly polishing these magnificent autos. Each booth had smartly dressed men on hand to point out new features and to answer questions. Some of these companies hired very attractive women to grace their area. There would be engine or transmission cuts-outs on display to show the inner workings, always nicely chrome plated. The year (1938–I think) that Oldsmobile came out with the hydromatic transmission, the cut-out for this new technology attracted rapt attention. And of course each display had tables loaded with glossy colored brochures free for the taking. And I did. My arms were loaded by the end of the day. When I got home I poured over these for many days afterward.

834 N. Marion Street, Oak Park, Illinois Early in second grade we moved from Chicago to Oak Park, the first suburb directly west of Chicago, about two miles from our former apartment on Monroe Street and about a mile north. Oak Park was a rectangle bounded by North Avenue on the north, Austin Boulevard on the east, Roosevelt Road on the south and Harlem Avenue on the west side. At that time 63,000 people lived in Oak Park. Most of the men worked in Chicago, many downtown somewhere. My impression was that very few of the wives and mothers worked outside the home. This was the 1930s and '40's before the war. My further impression was that lots of these well-to-do women went downtown to shop at stores like Marshall Fields, and Carson Pirie Scott on many days, and had their purchases delivered out to Oak Park to their houses by the stores. Commuting to downtown and to other Chicago locations was by the elevated train, either the Lake Street "L" or the Garfield. Some used the Northwestern steam train, which in Oak Park ran above and parallel to the Lake Street

"L." Of course one could drive, but parking was a problem, always in paid commercial lots. We took the car on our occasional trips into the city–either down Washington Boulevard or Jackson. Getting into the busy downtown streets between the tall sky scrapers was always a thrill to me as I sat in the back seat with my eyes glued to the window. The climax was always the drive along the lake shore.

My grade school was Horace Mann. I would walk to and from school alone at first, but later with Ricky Gill, my friend who lived three houses south of me on Marion Street. I have a few memories of grade school at Horace Mann which stand out. One was in the spring when our class went outside the building with drawing paper and crayons. We knelt down on the sidewalk putting our papers on the walk and drawing pictures. I remember the week of Thanksgiving when all of us had brought canned goods to give to the poor during a special all-school program. Each class processed down the stairways to the gym singing "Come Ye Thankful People, Come," as we dutifully carried our cans to the assembly. One year at the end of the year we had a picnic in the park across the street from the school. My mother had made egg salad sandwiches for me and I can still remember how good they tasted as all of us sat on the grass for our lunch. My most unhappy times were in gym class. I was not good at athletic activities and that must have become obvious to my class-mates for I was always, it seems, the last one chosen when we chose up sides for one game or another.

Ricky and I were fast friends and played together four seasons of the year, most of the time outside, but once in a while inside. Sometimes our play was with other kids on the block. Eugene Bercham from the house next door to mine and Louis Foster from down the street. There were one or two girls whose names I forget. One, I think was Carolyn. She lived a few houses down the block and across the street.

But most of the time it was Ricky and I who played together. Five vacant lots in a row across the street from my house provided a wonderful place to play. Part of the area had trees and shrubs which we called our woods, and the other part of the property was covered with grass and weeds which we called our prairie.

The 800 block of Marion Street was our playground. There were cement sidewalks on both sides of the street and the street was paved with asphalt between cement curbs with driveways beside each house leading to a backyard garage. Without much traffic in those days and very few cars parked on the street, we could have softball games on the street. But after supper in the dusk of evening we played other games like "kick the can." Or sometimes a few of us would sit on the curb and talk. And who knows what ideas those consultations hatched for other activities on the street! In the early days during hot summers we were delighted when th horse drawn ice wagon would come by slowly, slow enough for us to hop aboard and snatch a small piece of melting ice to suck on. As I remember it, this was alright with the ice man, but not with our parents who, in those days, were fearful that such activity might lead to polio, still much of a threat in the 1930s. A few years later, summer in the street brought the Good Humor truck, and this led to quick trips into the house to muster up a nickel for a an ice cream bar. But I also remember being alone on my front porch during rainstorms when dark clouds blanketed the street and the wind blew amid thunder and lightning. I would pretend that my porch was a ship as I watched the heavy rain pelting the street, which I imagined to be the ocean.

Eighth grade graduation in June of 1941was a big event, and then the next fall I entered Oak Park River Forest Township High School. In the fall of 1942 we moved from the Marion Street house because the owner sold it. We found a first floor apartment in a two flat building in south Oak Park.

338 So. Oak Park Avenue. From that point on. I was isolated from anyone else in the new neighborhood and my connection with the old neighborhood came to an end as did my relationship with Ricky Gill, unill much later in life.

A number of times during the summers of 1933 and 1934 my parents and I visited the World's Fair in Chicago, called *A Century of Progress.* I remember the various displays and shops of other countries. My mother liked the one from Czechoslovakia. My favorite display was the Transportation Building with all sorts of trains, trucks, and cars.

The key "signature" of the Fair was a streamlined train running on tracks above the fair carrying visitors from one end of the grounds to the other. My parents bought me a little toy bus modeled after the one which ran on the ground at the Fair.

As I think of it now, it appears to me that leaving our house on Marion Street and connections with Ricky Gill and the neighborhood, together with graduating from Horace Mann, signaled the end of childhood for me.

My parents and I made at least two out-of-town visits to my grand parents each year. My father's parents lived in the family home in Iowa, 240 miles away. My mother's parents lived in Missouri, a 300 mile journey.

<u>Ft. Madison, Iowa</u> I have fond memories of our family visits to my grandparents in Ft. Madison, Iowa. Ft. Madison is on the Mississippi River 240 miles southwest of Chicago. My parents would load up whatever car we had at the time and we would head down U.S. 34, oftentimes crossing the Mississippi at Burlington, Iowa, but many times we would drive south on the Illinois side and cross at Ft. Madison. What a thrill for me it was to cross over on the very long bridge over the very wide river and onto land again on the other side in Iowa after what seemed like a very long trip!

Grandma and Grandpa lived in a delightful big two-story frame house with a large yard, at 1320 Avenue I. It was an unpaved dirt street with a single train track down the middle. I believe it was once a day when a short train would come rumbling past the house–a locomotive, at first steam with a coal car, and later diesel, and perhaps one or two freight cars and a caboose–with a huge amount of noise and shaking of the very earth under my feet. What a thrill. Grandpa called it "The Doodlebug. Sometimes we would put a penny or a stick pin on the rail well before the train was close. After the train had passed the penny would be thin, smooth and twice the size it had been and the stick pin flat and an eighth of an inch wide, looking to me like a tiny sword.

My memories of my grandparents house, and yard remain quite vivid and most appealing. As you entered the house you stepped up onto a front porch and came to the front door on the front left hand side of the porch. The door opened into a small hallway with a stairway on the left leading up to the second floor. On the right was a door leading into a formal parlor. The one thing I remember about that room was the wind-up Victrola. The one record I remember was "La Paloma." I don't remember very many occasions when the family used this rather austere room.

At the foot of the stairs against the wall on the left was a small table which held a black enameled round powder puff box with a music box inside. I loved to listen to that magical music when I lifted off the cover. This music box belonged to Lena.

Our earliest visits were before any of my aunts were married and so they still lived at home. Harvey was also home much of the time, until later when his train routes kept him away. My uncle Leland was married and lived in Concord, Michigan. Adelaide was the first daughter to marry and move away. She married Carl Andres.

I remember Harvey's little room at the back of the house, upstairs next to the bathroom. My grandparents' bedroom was large, occupying the right side of a long hall. I remember it as very sunny with a huge rag rug. There must have been three or four other bedrooms up there, which I don't remember, except that at the very front was a sewing room, possibly attached to a bedroom. The long upstairs hall had a second stairway at the rear of the house, at the bottom of which was a small bathroom. This is where I remember Grandpa standing at a tiny wash basin before a mirror all lathered and shaving. This stairway opened into a good-sized kitchen, big enough to hold a wooden table and chairs in its center.

The back door was located in the far corner of the kitchen. Another door went out onto a screened-in porch on the north side of the house. I remember one time when my father and grandfather were sitting in the dark of the evening on a hot summer night on the little side porch. The only light I could see was the orange glowing ember of Grandpa's cigar! I had never seen him with a cigar before that, or since. Perhaps sensing my surprise, he explained. "This is to keep the mosquitos away."

The kitchen opened into a rather large sitting room on the right and a dining room on the left. A short hall led from the sitting room to the front door area of the house connecting to the front hallway.

I remember family gatherings in the sitting room, the pungent smell of steak and onions carried from the kitchen to the family assembled around the dining room table, and Grandpa and Grandma napping after lunch on couches in the sitting room.

A bedtime ritual for me was often promoted–I think--by Harvey. When everyone was standing around in the kitchen by the sitting room door, I was given the assignment of identifying each of my aunts. I was held –later led–to face each one and say the correct name. Lena! Adelaide!, Alice! Fern! To this day I can still see each smiling face in my mind's eye. This was the time when my father and others each would take an apple from a dish on the refrigerator to eat before bed time.

I remember Carl's exuberant deep voice and Adelaide's accompanying smile, Lena's more reticent nature, Fern's quiet smiles and one particular remark of Alice's after she and Glenn were married. She said one evening around the kitchen doorway something like this. "I just like so much those tiny tools Glenn uses in his work–little screwdrivers and wrenches." Another time Harvey came up with a unique surmise which has stuck in my mind. "I just imagine there are wooden pencils labeled *American*. Just about everything has a variety called *American*." I'm sorry, but I have little memory of Leland and Sally, except that I think he was quite slender and Sally wasn't!

I remember Grandma as a tall woman, very gentle and quiet. I have an enlargement of a four generations snapshot hanging in my office with Grandma seated in a lawn chair outdoors holding Doris's and my first child, Ross, who was about a year old at the time. Standing on her left was my father, and I am standing on her right. I think the picture was taken in Andres' back yard in Peoria at a time when we visited Carl and Adelaide. That was taken about 1957, I think. Of the four Krebills in that scene, I am the only one now alive.

My grandpa was also gentle and somewhat quiet; yet he would tell me things as we walked about his yard and in his garage. One characteristic of his speech was the use of the word "idee" with the emphasis on the first syllable, instead of idea.

In my later years I have grown to see and appreciate the quiet gentleness in the Krebill family a trait which I have come to realize is a legacy of our Mennonite heritage. To me this heritage is one of peace and non-violence, a certain non-competitiveness, and a reticence when it comes to putting one's self forward. This is an appealing trait which has been passed to succeeding generations as well, I think.

By the time of our family visits to Ft. Madison, Grandpa and Grandma's family membership was in St. John's Evangelical Church in Ft. Madison. Earlier they had been members of the Mennonite church in Donnelson. I have vague memories of going to church at St. John's when our visits included a Sunday.

Grandpa was retired the whole time I knew him. He and his brother, who was known to us as Uncle Ed, were partners in a grain mill in Ft. Madison, which had been sold to a large milling company and no longer was in use. I have a vague recollection of being shown the building. Also in the neighborhood of the mill were piles of clam shells from the nearby Mississippi, which were riddled with holes. These were left overs from a button making plant in which buttons had been cut out of clam shells. In this area of town near the river there was often an acrid odor from a mill which made paper.

Extending from the backdoor of the house to the garage at the very back of the lot was a mature Concord grape arbor, creating a tunnel leading back to the garage. The many vines not only filled in both sides but the area overhead as well. This was an enticing place, especially when bunches of dark blue grapes hung down from overhead and on the sides as well.

Also between the garage and the house in the center of a grassy area was a very large and ancient pear tree. It too produced delicious fruit in late summer.

As you faced the garage to the left of the grape arbor a long unpaved driveway connected the street to the an open parking area in front of the garage door. Vehicles would turn right to enter the garage.

On the other side of the driveway across from the house was an undeveloped lot with Grandpa's vegetable garden on the back half of the area. The part of the garden which stands out in my memory was Grandpa's compost pit in the midst of the vegetable plants. It was an open scar in the soil into which he put kitchen scraps, such items as melon peelings and egg shells. Without knowing it, Grandpa was an organic gardener as was everyone else in those days, I suppose. Between the garden and the street was a grassy area. This was the favorite place for children to play.

Grandpa let us play in his rather large two wheeled garden cart, which I assume he had built using metal farm implement wheels, probably around three feet in diameter. As I remember I think the box would have been about three by four feet with foot and half sides. It was pushed like a wheel barrow. I would always have to persuade someone to push me around in it.

Most always I was the only grandchild visiting, but a few years later after Adelaide and Carl were married, their oldest daughter, Audrey, would be in Ft. Madison with her parents for a visit at the same time as our visit. A few times, Leland and Sally with their two children, Granger and Sally, would be there on a visit. These were especially happy times for me, to be able to play with cousins. It would have been much later when Alice and Glenn visited with Betty, but I do have a fleeting memory of Betty, when she was a little girl, when I was in high school. By that time only Lena would have been at home, for Fern would have moved to Washington, D.C. and Harvey would have been living elsewhere in connection with his railway postal mail route.

The most intriguing place of all for me was Grandpa's garage–his shop. I can still smell the wonderful combination of oil and grease soaked into the dirt floor along with the smell of ancient wood, leather, automotive parts and who knows what else! A huge wooden work bench littered with tools, and all sorts of interesting things piled up, or hung up all over the place! The most unusual instrument for me was the two-handled pipe threader.

On my first visits as a young child, Grandpa had a large four-door Nash automobile. My guess now is that it was about a 1928 vintage.

It was tan in color and the most interesting thing about it for me was how the engine was locked and how the driver prepared to turn on the engine. In the center of the front seat floor next to the gear shift was a little protruding cylinder into which the driver put the key to unlock the transmission so that he could start the engine. Or, at least I think it was the transmission which was to be locked with the key, instead of the ignition as in cars since that time. I loved to go for rides with Grandpa in his big car. I am reminded now of a emory reported to me by a shirt-tail relative–whose family had done the genealogy which we now have. "I can remember," she said, "seeing Pete Krebill driving the first motor car in Ft. Madison, an E.M.F, an open air auto loaded with his kids." This points, I think, to the origin of Grandpa's, my father's, and Harvey's unusually intense love of the automobile. A love which I must admit, I have always shared.

Sometime along the line, the Nash was traded in for a 1937 Ford four sedan, shiny black "streamlined" car, which I can still see parked in the Nash' place in the garage.

Harvey was such a lover of Fords. No other car could compare. I remember one trip when my father had had to borrow my Uncle Otto's (on my mother's side) Chevrolet to make the trip to Ft. Madison. When Harvey saw it, he was unrestrained in his disdain for that car. It was, I think, a 1938 model with some unusual decorative chrome on the doors, which Harvey pointed to and muttered "What's that for?"

I wonder if Grandpa's succession of license plates still hangs on the inside wall of his garage shop? (Now owned by someone else) How I used to look at those plates covering the years he drove a car. I wonder what year was on the last one. So far as I know these plates were always dark blue and white-–numerals and background colors reversed from year to year.

And, by the way, if you had looked into my garage you coud have seen a succession of licence plates hanging on my wall, beginning with a 1945 Illinois plate made of heavy fabric. (It was during the WW II years when metal was reserved for the war effort.) There was a succession of Wyoming plates-- County 7–Goshen County (Yoder and Hawk Springs.) And two successions of Montana plates: No. 3 for Yellowstone County (Billings) and 6 for Gallatin County (Bozeman).

There is much about Ft. Madison which I do not remember. But so far as I was concerned, Grandpa and Grandma's house and yard made up, for me, a magic kingdom.

My, oh my, I wish I could go back in time and visit Pete and Ida Krebill in their house on Ave. "I" in Ft. Madison, Lee County (No. 51) Iowa

St. Louis, Missouri At least once a year my parents and I visited my maternal grandparents in St. Louis. This would be a trip to the south west of Chicago on Route 66. After six or seven long hours we would finally come to the Mississippi River. It was always a thrill to cross over to Missouri on the "Chain of Rocks Bridge." The bridge brought us to St. Louis and emptied into an industrial area along the river-front through which we drove south on Broadway, I think. And then we went up a steep hill on College Avenue to St. James Evangelical Church on the right side with the parsonage just beyond, the home of Grandma and Grandpa, and in the earlier years also the home of my uncle Otto. The parsonage was a rather large two-story brick rectangular building. I don't remember exactly the floor plan completely. The kitchen and dining room were side by side at the back with a full porch with a door into each room. There was a family room and a parlor, which was rarely used, except for pastoral calls which my grandfather received. I believe I was told that my parents were married by my grandfather in this room. Since their marriage was so soon after my mother's sister, Clara, had died, a big church wedding was not considered appropriate. My grandfather's study and at least four bedrooms were upstairs. I slept alone in one of the bedrooms at the front facing the street. I remember the old dark green window shades which had tiny holes here and there. In the dark these seemed to me to be like stars. On hot and humid nights when the windows were open, I remember hearing the calls of a street peddler. "Hot Tamales. . . Hot Tamales. . . Hot Tamales," as he wheeled down the street.

Mealtimes in the dining room are ingrained in my memory. I especially remember the old green tea pot with gold decoration in which Grandma used a combination of black and green tea. A couple of times when I was reluctant to eat my meal, Grandpa would step into the long hall next to the dining room and take an empty mailing tube to use as a megaphone to call in a deep mysterious voice, "Eat your platter clean! " This was in the 1930s, not long after the Great Depression, when President Hoover coined that phrase as an encouragement to Americans in hard times.

The parsonage was perhaps twenty feet from the large brick church building. This was paved in cement as a driveway to what I think was a free standing one car garage in the back yard. I remember my father and Otto washing their cars in the driveway using a hose on very hot days. I don't think Otto owned a car but was washing Grandpa's 1934 Plymouth gray sedan. There was hardly any front yard, but an extensive back yard surrounded by a tall board fence, beyond which was an alley. When I was quite small I used to be afraid of the boogey man on the other side of the fence. The yard was in grass except for some flower beds around the borders. I remember playing in a wagon in the yard with my cousins, Ted and Richard, who lived in Webster Groves, a suburb of St. Louis.

At the rear, of the church building, there was a newer building in which here was a combination gymnasium and auditorium and a bowling alley. I don't think this new building was attached to the original church building. In the area in front of the new building were sidewalks and grassy places. I remember one time in the fall when my grandmother and a number of other ladies of the church were making apple butter in a large kettle . At other times the women of the church sat at frames making quilts. I'm not sure where these were, perhaps in the gym. In the newer building was a room devoted to mimeographing. Grandpa sometimes took me into that room and I can still remember the aroma of the ink which permeated the room

Many times when we visited in St. Louis in the summer there would be a family picnic in Forest Park with Ted and Richard and their parents, Theodore and Viola, as well as my grandparents and Otto. These were always enjoyable times, since that sort of activity was infrequent in our life in Chicago.

I remember a time or two when we visited my mother's Uncle Jacob and Aunt Lucy Schoening (possibly related to Doris's Shoening relatives) Braun and their children in Webster Groves. It was a most unusual experience for me to be with a family with so many children. The oldest was Ted, followed by his sister Dorothy, and then Harold, Eugene and Marian. I remember one particular evening when each of the children played a different instrument and together made a sort of family orchestra. Ted played the bass violin and Harold played the oboe, but I don't remember what the other instruments were. But it made quite an impression upon me.

Eugene (Gene) was my age and so when Ted and Richard were also visiting we four would play together. At the time of my grandfather's funeral, it must have been decided that we were too young to attend, and so all four of us spent the time playing at Gene's house.

St. Louis was the headquarters of the Evangelical Church, which accounted for the cluster of relatives in the area. Uncle Theodore was the editor of the official magazine of the Evangelical church, "The Messenger." Mother's Uncle Jacob was Secretary of Home Missions for the Denomination. Both men had offices in St. Louis. Webster Groves was the location of the Evangelical Church's Eden Seminary.

<u>Visiting Aunt Martha and Uncle Ralph</u> My parents and I also made trips occasionally to visit my mother's sister and her husband, Aunt Martha and Uncle Ralph. Ralph Weiser was an Evangelical pastor. I remember four of his locations over the years: Wabash, Indiana, Milwaukee, Wisconsin, Cape Girardeau, Missouri, and Minneapolis, Minnesota. My only memory of Wabash is an image of Ralph's study in the parsonage, in which he and my father often visited.. I was quite small when we went to Milwaukee and don't remember much except that we rode in Ralph and Martha's Model A Ford, a 1930 or '31 coupe. Aunt Martha named it "Henrietta" as the feminine version of Henry Ford. Two memories come clear to me about our visit to Cape Girardeau. The enticing aroma of toast when I came down for breakfast, a breakfast in which our family ws introduced to honey dew melon for the first time. The other memory is of Martha playing the pipe organ in the church building when we were given a tour during the week. My only memory of Minneapolis was how Martha and Ralph raved over

how different that part of the country was with so many unfamiliar names. For most, if not all of those years, Ralph and Martha did not have children. At some point in their lives, they adopted a baby girl, whom they named Lois. I think this may have been during their life in Buffalo, New York, where they lived after Minnesota. I was happy to hear that I had a new girl cousin.

Union Station in Downtown Chicago Every so often I had a chance go see an uncle when he came to Chicago by train in connection with his work. Sometimes this wask when my Uncle Theodore to town. More often it was my mother's Uncle Jacob. He always referred to his suitcase as his grip. My father's brother, Harvey, also came occasionally. These trips to Union Station were always a thrill to me, especially when we walked out onto the covered platform and walked along side the trains which had just arrived.

But most of my life as a child was spent in our nuclear family of three, for the most part without contact with extended family members. It would be much later when I experienced having brothers, aunts, uncles, and cousins around all the time, when I became an adopted member of Doris's extended family in LaSalle, Illinois.

PART 3

GROWING UP

Throughout my high school years my social context was the youth group in First Presbyterian Church of Oak Park called TUXIS, and particularly my friendship with John Jones in the group who lived a few blocks south of me. We regularly walked to church on Sunday evenings for TUXIS. At other times in the week we met to go to a soda fountain for Green Rivers sodas and lots of talk .

<u>Oak Park River Forest Township High School</u> In many ways high school itself is not very memorable. Neither a particularly bad experience nor an especially good one. Just good preparation for college. I took a lot of math, partly because my father was a math teacher. A couple of the advanced courses gave me some college credit, which I never used. I had a course in drafting which I think must have been required. It was in a far corner of the building and it took a long time to get into the drafting room. I don't think I did very well in that course, but gained a knowledge of engineering and architectural drawing. Typing was another course in which I did not do well. In fact I think the teacher, who was a friend of my Uncle Otto's fudged a bit to pass me. Worst of all was swimming which I did not pass, but was granted reluctant approval by the swim coach. The gymnasium and swimming pools were in a separate building in the block south of the main building. To get there we had to walk through a fairly long tunnel.

As I remember it, some of the English history and social studies classes were more to my liking. I also enjoyed choral music and by my senior year I was in some sort of advanced choir, which sang elsewhere in the community on occasion. This also involved singing in the chorus of the Gilbert and Sullivan operetta, HMS Pinafore.

TUXIS, on the other hand was an extremely good experience, not only with its regular Sunday evening meetings, but for the many social times friends from the group gathered for activities outside of church. Sometimes at one of their homes. Never in mine however.

Random memories come back to life from those four years. Summer nights on the edge of Lake Michigan, seated on the grass in the crowd in front of the Grant Park band shell listening to the Grant park orchestra with my close friends from the the TUXIS group. The same group in one of the member's living room playing games--one about a spoon by which to identify someone. Sunset over Lake Michigan at Saugatuck, Michigan at Westminster Lodge, High School camp–Vespers, singing "Day is Dying in the West." Coming away from Communion in the darkness at camp, feeling the presence of God.

<u>The Oak Park Arms Hotel</u> A very significant and influential component in my growing up was the Oak Park Arms Hotel and my job there as bell-hop. From the very beginning of my work in the hotel I was quite taken with the "feel" of working in a hotel. Even before my job at the Arms, I remember going to dinner with my parents at another hotel in Oak Park, The Carlton. I can still feel the intrigue of imagining what it would be like to work there.

We lived at 338 So. Oak Park avenue, two doors from Washington Boulevard across which, on the corner of Washington and Oak Park the Oak Park Arms was located, at 408 So. Oak Park Avenue. It was during the war when the young men who had been bell-hops had gone into the military service leaving "Pop" Weber as the head bell-man without much help. He gave me a job at the beginning of my Sophomore year in High school, first as an elevator operator and then as a bell-hop. Pop Weber advised me to confront all problems brought up by guests with "I dunno nuttin bout it."

I enjoyed the hotel and my part-time job after school and on the week-ends. My usual shift was from 4 PM to midnight, though sometimes on the week ends from 8 to 4. This consisted mainly of carrying the bags of guests who were checking in and some who were checking out, as well as other services such as sending out laundry and dry cleaning. Running a coat check room was a major part of the work especially on the week ends when the Arms had quite a number of wedding dinners and receptions. I continued to work at the Arms part-time as my school schedule permitted for the next nine years, until after seminary graduation.

Emhurst College, Elmhurst, Illinois During the summer of 1945 My parents and I took a trip to Urbana, Illinois to get me enrolled in the University of Illinois. This was an experience which got nowhere. After being given a mimeographed sheet listing all the housing possibilities and being instructed to go and find one, I became discouraged at the huge impersonal nature of what attending there would entail. That was the end of my pre-enrollment. We returned to Oak Park and made another trip, this time to Elmhurst College, eight miles west of Oak Park. We went to seek Dean Mueller in his office, a man whom my parents knew. Both my grandfather Braun and my father had been students at Elmhurst. Along with Eden Seminary it was a focal point for many of the families connected with the Evangelical Church at the time. I was very rapidly accepted and given a room assignments in Irion Hall. In the Fall I began my college career, moving in to Irion Hall. Very shy and apprehensive I moved into my room and would later meet my room mate, Jack Branding from Chicago.

fter my parents left to return to Ok Park I went down to the Irion lounge where Lyndon Schaefferly, also a new freshman student was playing the piano. This seemed to draw the group of us gathered there together. From that day on college was a rich and full, pleasurable and rewarding experience for me. You might say that those four great years gave me my adult life. And my wife!

The pleasures of college life centered around the group of us who lived in Iron Hall, the only mens dorm at the time. Aside from Irion there was Senior Lodge, which was a house in which seven or eight boys lived, among whom was my cousin, Ted Braun, a year ahead of me. South Hall was the only women's dorm. All on-campus students ate in the Commons, which served three meals a day cafeteria style without, however, any choices.

With a total enrollment of only 290 students the first semester of my freshman year, we all knew each other, at least casually. We knew the other members of our own class much more fully.

With the ending of World War II, veterans began coming to Elmhurst, eventually doubling the enrollment. Many of these were freshmen who integrated into our class quite easily. These men were a bit more serious, one indication of which was their refusal to take part in the customary hazing of freshmen by upperclass students.

Doris Schoening was among the women in the freshman class in 1945 at Elmhurst, living in South Hall. She had graduated from LaSalle-Peru (Illinois) High School in 1943. Following graduation, she went to work in the office of the Westclox Corporation in Peru, in the payroll department. She lived at home at 860 O" Connor Avenue in LaSalle and commuted to work by city bus. She worked for Westclox for two years before entering Elmhurst College in the fall of 1945 at the recommendation of her pastor, Rev. Walter Kleffmann. She had earlier been tempted to go to Moody Bible Institute in Chicago where some of her Joop cousins were attending. Had Rev. Kleffman not succeeded in this important bit of pastoral advice, Doris would not have been in this narrative. But as it turned out, he performed our marriage later!

There are two stories about how Doris and I first met. One is that we met each other in library one evening when we were both looking for an English translation of a story we had been assigned in German class. The other was that Clint Hageman, a fellow classmate in Irion Hall and I were looking out of his window in Irion Hall one afternoon when we spotted Doris Schoening and Kathy Meyers going to the tennis court in Wilder Park across the street. Clint said, "Look at that cute little Doris Schoening. Let's go and invite ourselves to play doubles with them."

That's what we did. Clint chose to play on Doris' side, leaving me on Kathy's side. But the result was that Doris and I fell in love and later we were married.

I took Doris on our first date to the Spinning Wheel restaurant in Downers Grove on Ogden Avenue. For this grand occasion I borrowed my Dad's car. Throughout the rest of our college years Doris and I dated, often walking downtown to the movies at the York Theater and then to Keeler's restaurant next door where we had some kind of snack afterward. Doris often ordered an olive nut sandwich, something I never tried.

I was involved in four extra-curricular activities during my college years. I was advertising mnager for the Exponent, the weekly campus newspaper. Later I became manager of a newly formed wired radio broadcasting station, WRS, which grew out of a war-surplus Army radar trailer given to the college. A few tech savvy students had pulled enough parts out of the trailer to build a broadcasting instrument capable to sending signals on wires to the two dorms.

For the last two years I served as vice president of our Class of 1949. My good friend, George Langeler, was president. For three years George and I co-directed the Student-Faculty show, which featured acts by both students and faculty members.

In June of 1949 Doris and I each received our Bachelor of Arts degree: mine with a major in sociology and a minor in psychology and Doris's in Christian Education.

Chicago, Illinois After graduation Doris went to work in downtown Chicago, first for Scripture Press, then for the Elmer J. Engle Company. During college she had done housework for the Elmer Engle family a few blocks south of the college on Prospect Avenue. Mr. Engle hired her to work for him in the office of his business. He was a manufacturer's representative for Foster-Grant. She lived at the McCormick Y.W.C.A. on Oak between State and Dearborn. I rode the Clark Street Street-car to visit her.

McCormick Theological Seminary-Chicago In the fall of 1949 I began my three years at McCormick, then located on the tri-corner of Fullerton, Halsted and Lincoln, which was only a walking distance from Lincoln Park and the lake. I roomed with my college friend, Joe Degi, in McCormick Hall and we went through our seminary experience together. Very soon we found ourselves part of a small prayer group which became a life-long fellowship group as well. Oscar Hussel emerged as the natural leader of the group, his roommate, Bill Johnson, Chet Wetzel, Neal Perz, and Bob Lodwick made up the group. During the seminary years, all of us except Neal married. With the exception of Neal, who dropped completely out of touch after seminary all of us and our respective spouses have remained in continual communication ever since.

While I had high regard for all of my professors, two were perhaps most influential: Hulda Niebuhr in Christian Education, and Joseph Haroutunian in Systematic Theology. The others were certainly memorable and contributed significantly to my thought and practice of ministry in the years following.

I continued to work at the Oak Park Arms on week-ends and during the summer which helped me significantly to be debt-free and without having had to depend upon my parents for both college and seminary.

In May of 1952 commencement exercises were held in Fourth Presbyterian Church where I was awarded a Bachelor of Divinity degree. This later was renamed, Master of Divinity.

PART 4

MARRIAGE

Our Wedding in La Salle, Illinois. On August 19, Doris and I were married in Trinity United Church of Christ in LaSalle, Illinois. This had been the church in which Doris was baptized, grew up and was confirmed. The Rev. Walter Kleffmann performed the marriage. Lila Denny was matron of honor, John Jones was best man. Garnet Vyduna and Dolores West were Doris's attendants. Bill Schoening and George Langeler were my attendants. It was a beautiful ceremony which included three songs given by Doris's cousin, Aurelia, and our friend from college, Walt Krebs played the organ. A reception followed in the fellowship hall of the church.

Our Honeymoon trip to Gatlinburg, Tennessee. We drove to the Great Smoky Mountain National Park for our honeymoon. We used my father's Studebaker Champion. We spent the first night at a downtown hotel in Bloomington, Illinois. The next day was Sunday. We went to church in Nashville before driving on to Gatlinburg where we stayed at the New Gatlinburg Inn for the rest of our time in the Smoky's. We enjoyed driving int the Park and in the evenings visiting the cafes which featured mountain music. On our return trip we bought a gallon of apple cider which blew up in the heat of our car. On our way through Kentucky we stopped to take an underground tour of Mammoth Cave.

PART 5

ADULTHOOD

Our marriage marked the beginning of full adulthood and again my memories emerge from the various places we lived.

McCormick Hall-2330 No. Halsted St. Chicago, Ill. Due to the explosive growth in the numbers of married students, during the summer of our marriage the Seminary converted McCormick from a men's dormitory into a dorm for married students. At first nothing was done to alter the building except to designate the one bathroom on each floor either for men or for women. We had a third floor room. Doris had her bathroom on our floor. I had to climb up very steep stairs to the fourth floor for mine.

One further alteration to the building came as a result of a fire which broke out in our room one evening when Doris and I were using two or three electrical appliances which we had gotten as wedding gifts. This turned out to be too much for the antiquated electrical system in the building, consisting of merely two places where a light bulb wall socket was located. Oscar Hussel rushed down the hall, grabbed a fire extinguisher and doused our fire. As a result the Seminary set aside one room on each floor in which a heavier circuit was installed for ironing and a limited amount of cooking.

Fowler Hall was located not far from McCormick Hall on the campus. During the summer between my middler and senior years Doris and I were moved to Fowler Hall. Though I did not have classes during the summer we lived on campus while Doris continued to work in the Loop and I worked at the Oak Park Arms Hotel for the summer. Other than that I do not remember anything about our months in Fowler.

Dayton Apartments, owned by the seminary were located a block south of the seminary on the east side of Dayton Street. For my senior year we lived in a second floor one-room apartment. In the small living room, a wall-mounted apartment kitchen unit held a small refrigerator and cooking range. On the opposite wall were folding doors behind which a Murphy In-a-door Bed was mounted. Held upright on one end by a massive spring, the bed was pulled down for use and then returned to the enclosure behind the doors during the day. A very small bathroom and clothes closet were located off the living room as well.

A tiny grocery store was situated in the basement of an apartment a half a block north of us on the other side of Dayton on the corner of Webster Street. We made good use of what the young man who owned it had to offer since we now prepared all three meals in our apartment, for the first time in our married lives. I don't remember much more about Dayton except that I was frequently teased by my friends for driving to the campus for classes–only a block and half. By this time we were the proud owners of the 1940 Studebaker Champion which my father had sold to us. It was the car he had loaned to us for our honeymoon to the Smoky's.

Fourth Presbyterian Church-Chicago, Illinois. In the evening of May 8, 1952, our senior class sat in the front four or five pews of Fourth Presbyterian Church on Michigan Avenue garbed in our caps and gowns. We were the graduating class of McCormick Seminary, having completed the required courses over the previous three academic years. Wives, parents, and others filled the sanctuary behind us on that pivotal day of our lives.

First Presbyterian Church-Oak Park, Illinois. The Presbytery of Chicago met in my home church on the evening of May 16, 1952, to ordain me as a Minister of the Gospel in the Presbyterian Church in the U.S.A. and thus to become a member of the Presbytery of Chicago. Technically I was ordained as an "Evangelist" because at that point I did not have a "call" to a particular position. Such a call would be issued to me later that Summer from the Presbytery of Casper in Wyoming. The act of ordination involved the "laying on of hands" by the members of the Presbytery of Chicago present for this service. Much to my mother's chagrin, her brother, my Uncle, the Rev. Theodore C. Braun, was not invited to participate in the Laying of Hands even though he had given the ordination prayer in the service. He was a minister of the United Church of Christ and not a member of Chicago Presbytery.

I remember three of the ministers of Chicago Presbytery who took part in my ordination. Allen Hjerpe, Moderator of Presbytery, Luther Stein, pastor of my home church, First Presbyterian Church of Oak Park, and William C. Graham, pastor of Morgan Park Presbyterian Church, who had been assistant pastor at Oak Pak First when I was growing up. I think Dr. Stein preached the sermon and Bill Graham gave the charge to the newly ordained pastor. The only words I remember from the service were from Graham in his charge–*Paul, preach the whole Gospel."* Over the years since I have come to see the meaning in this. One is not to be selective in what one reads and preaches from the Bible. Don't emphasize the same message over and over again. This day of my ordination was especially precious to my mother.

Not many days later Doris and I loaded up our car, a black four-door 1940 DeSoto, and a utility trailer I had bought from Sears for the occasion, and began our trek to Wyoming.

For me, the West was characterized by Colorado and Denver. And so we began our trip by going to St. Louis to participate in John Schroeder's marriage to Maxine. We then drove to Denver. This took two or three days. At one of the motels, when we checked in I was told "You can park your trailer over here, Sonny." I found that rather deflating since I thought of ourselves as full grown adults beginning a very grown up phase of our lives.

We passed through Denver and headed north on US 85 through Cheyenne north to Hawk Springs which was about 83 miles. Not too far out of Cheyenne we stopped the car to look at a panorama neither of us had ever seen. Nothing of human construction except the road itself. In all 360 degrees, just rolling fields of grassland under a bright blue sky. And we were only an hour or so from where we would be living. We passed through Hawk Springs without stopping and up ten more miles to Yoder, which is two miles west of the highway. We drove into town and found a Conoco gas station and garage and asked the attendant where we could find the Fred Splinter residence. He pointed us to a house we could see about a block away. When we got to the house Mrs. Splinter came out and greeted us excitedly. "Rev. Krebill," which she pronounced Kraybill. From that day forward our name has been pronounced, "Kraybill" as it had been in my father's youth–the true German pronunciation, I believe now that my parents had changed it to "Krebill" during the 1920s in an attempt to downplay our German heritage, a not uncommon attempt in the World War I era. Thus began our Wyoming days which would continue through May of 1956. As I think about my name pronunciation change, it occurs to me that this change marked the new life I would now live, having left my youth behind.

Yoder and Hawk Springs, Wyoming

1952-1956 Pastor of the Presbyterian Community Churches of Yoder and Hawk Springs, Wyoming–Presbytery of Casper.

Our first home in Wyoming was the teacherage, both sides of it, on the west edge of Yoder. This was quite primitive by our standards. It was heated by gravity fed kerosene heating stoves, one on each side. Each had an overturned can which we had to fill from a large tank outside the house The house was built as two apartments, each with a living room, kitchen and bedroom. Between the two was a bathroom and a porch with a refrigerator shared by the two apartments.

I used one of the bedrooms for a study, in which I churned out a sermon and service for each week and whatever else I was to do. This included typing up a Sunday bulletin on a stencil which I mimeographed on an old A.B. Dick machine in the basement of the Yoder church

Alternating by the week as to which church would have the early worship. Sunday school was at 9:30 in each town, I think.

Each church had a monthly Session meeting and a monthly Women's Fellowship meeting.

After a year or so, the Hawk Springs church built a new manse for us to live in. Much of the fund raising for this came from a temporary café which the women opened on Main Street, especially during pheasant season in the fall when a lot of hunters from Cheyenne came up into our area.

I remember going to the lumber yard in LaGrange, ten miles south of Hawk Springs, with two or three of the elders to arrange for the owner of the yard to design and provide the building materials for the house. He told us that we didn't need an architect. He would design it. The men of the church built it entirely, except for the wiring and wet wall plastering which they hired. It was a one level three bedroom house on a cement slab around 1100 square feet in size with hardwood floors. It had a forced air propane-fired furnace with a well equipped kitchen. Really a very nice house.

After the house was completed, there was a rather lengthy delay until a well driller could come and drill for water. When water was found, and judged to be excellent soft water.

We had the minimum of furniture for the manse, which eventually included an overstuffed rocking chair given to us as a Christmas present by the Yoder church. We used a couple of wooden apple boxes, which had come with our stuff from Illinois for end tables in the living room. These have served us well in all the years since for various purposes including shelving for a stained glass studio in our home in Bozeman. (Given up recently when we sold our house to move to a retirement apartment in 2012)

Everything about our life in Wyoming was new to us and it would be impossible to describe it all. We learned the day-to-day work of a parish pastor as we went along and that seemed to develop effectively.

Calling on members of the congregation who were in the hospital became a fairly usual activity. For minor problems the hospital in Torrington was adequate, but more major needs required hospitalization in Scottsbluff, Nebraska, twenty five or so miles east, or in Cheyenne. I must admit that Doris and I enjoyed these further trips, which always meant eating in a restaurant before returning home.

Our introduction into Campus Ministry began in the fall of 1955 when I went to my mail box in Yoder and pulled out a letter from Paul McCleave, pastor of the First Presbyterian Church in Bozeman, Montana. In it he explained that the Presbyterians in Bozeman were applying to the national Board of Christian Education to establish and fund a full time campus ministry at Montana State College. He asked me if I would be interested in interviewing for the position of full time university pastor. I hastily read it and just as quickly rejected the idea. I took the letter home to show it to Doris. At that point the idea did not interest Doris either. But as was my custom, I didn't throw away the letter. I put it rather on the stack of stuff on my desk.

I believe God intervened and a few days later I re-read the request and this time we were interested. Meanwhile Dr. McCleave suffered a heart attack, delaying the process until after the first of the year.

I signified my interest, and in late February I was invited to Bozeman to an interview by the search committee.

On a very cold winter morning on February 28, 1956, I arrived on the Northern Pacific train in Bozeman after having driven to Casper, where I took the bus to Laurel, Montana. Staying overnight, I boarded the train the next morning. I carried my little suitcase off the train and began walking in the direction of downtown Bozeman. I was taken by surprise to find that the train station was not in the downtown business area, but rather many blocks north of Main Street. The ground was heavily covered with snow. A passing motorist picked me up and asked me where I was going. I told him I wanted to find a café. He dropped me off at a café on Main Street, most likely somewhere between Rouse and Bozeman streets.

I walked to the Babcock entrance of First Presbyterian Church. Betty McKean, the church secretary, met me at the door. She expressed surprise as she told me that they had expected; me the day before. She and Paul McCleave quickly made arrangements for the committee to meet in the Student Union Building of the college for lunch and an interview with me. As close as I can remember, the committee was made up of: Oscar Thomas from the range management department, Bob Seibel from electrical engineering, Jim Bassett from the Wool lab of MSC, Ora Lemon from the Christian Education Committee of the church, Paul Vischer, MD from the congregation, Helen Johnson from the congregation. All were active members of First Presbyterian Church. Paul McCleave led the meeting. We met in a room in the SUB and did not tour any of the campus. I do not remember anything from the interview, but the result of it was that they offered me the position at the conclusion of the meeting. I was ready to accept, but I do not remember if I accepted at that time or after returning home to discuss it with Doris. Most likely the latter.

At 3 PM I boarded the Greyhound bus to Laurel where I took the Burlington train to Casper and drove home to Hawk Springs. This process then, included at least one secret phone call to Paul McCleave which we made in a phone booth in Torrington so that no one on our party line could hear us.

The necessary arrangements were made during March and April for us to terminate our work in Yoder and Hawk Springs and for the move to Bozeman.

Bozeman, Montana would now be our home. In early May, the Mayflower moving van packed our furniture and possessions, including the upright piano the two congregations had given us. After it left we stayed overnight at Mabel and Oral Anders home, which was the first farm south of Hawk Springs on the the highway. After a great farm breakfast we left Anders home and the rest of our first parish to drive north on US 85, to Torrington and then to Casper and up to Billings. Then west to Bozeman, arriving in the evening at the Manse, McCleave's home on Cleveland and Third, which a few years later would come to be the Westminster Foundation manse, our home.

Our first residence was a second floor apartment in the Townhouse Apartments on South Tracy, which Paul McCleave had lined up for us. The movers brought our load there and had a very difficult time getting the piano into the basement of the building to be stored until we could have a place to put it. They had to turn it on end in order to move it down in that position.

The morning after moving into the Townhouse Apartments, I attended the eight o'clock student-led chapel service at Danforth Chapel on the campus. When I returned to the apartment, Doris had a tasty bacon, egg and toast breakfast waiting for us. This morning routine would continue on a five days a week basis for a number of months or so come. Thus began our eleven-year ministry on the camps of Montana State College, which a few years later was renamed Montana State University.

After a few months in the Townhouse, the Westminster Foundation rented a house at 703 So. 11th for us as a manse and as a place to entertain students.

In 1957, The local operating committee of the Westminster Foundation of the Synod of Montana, at Montana State College bought the manse from the First Presbyterian Church in Bozeman to be used as the Manse for the campus minister. The purchase price was $17,500.

I "inherited" the Westminster Club, a student fellowship which met for supper and a program each Sunday evening of the college year. The local session had organized this and Paul McCleave had been its advisor. I took over in May of 1956 with a few weeks remaining of the year. On one of those Sunday evenings the group took a trip to Butte for a picnic in the old Columbia Gardens. There must have been three or four carloads. We rode over with a student who served as a helpful guide to Doris and me. We were impressed by the fact that he had been a member of the Montana State Legislature.

The Westminster Foundation Program at MSC soon grew to include monthly married student Potluck suppers at the church followed with various programs, weekly study groups from time to time on assorted topics, individual counseling, and weekly Friday night open houses in our home for fellowship.

As the first full time campus pastor at Montana State, I worked alone the first few years until the Wesley foundation brought Gerry Thrush t work for the Methodists and the Lutheran Student Foundation brought Herb Strom to work with Lutherans. The three of us began to do some things together such as study groups. In the next few years St. Luke's Episcopal Church in Bozema provided campus ministry through a part-time priest and the Roman Catholic Diocese named a priest to campus work. We did some cooperative work with them as well.

My first office was provided by the local church. It was located on the upper floor of the education addition just west of the Babcock Street door. Later I was moved to a room on the main floor just south of the stairs at the south Willson entrance. Together with the other campus pastors we tried to get assigned to offices on the campus, but the staff in the student affairs department resisted our request not wanting us, to be established as part of the college. For a short time we were given temporary space in one of the Quonsets west of the heating plant. Later we were given a room in the basement hall of the SUB which we could share on a scheduled basis.

In 1962 this problem of location was finally resolved when the Lutherans, Episcopalians and Presbyterians, together bought a house across from the Lewis and Clark Dorms at 812 So. Eighth Street which was used for offices and programming. We named it the Campus Christian Center through which interdenominational and cooperative work became even more feasible and effective.

In 1962 my ministry was expanded when the United Campus Christian Ministry (UCCM) was organized at MSU, expanding the Presbyterian campus ministry in union with the United Churches of Christ, the American Baptist Churches and the Disciples of Christ churches in Montana. The Westminster Foundation board of the Synod was similarly expanded to become The Montana Ministries in Higher Education (MMHE).

During my campus ministry years I had a close unofficial relationship with First Presbyterian Church in Bozeman. This was most noticeable to the congregation and the public through my participation in the weekly worship as well as in occasional preaching. Frequently, when the pastor of the church was out of town for one reason or another, I was called upon to conduct the funeral of a church member. Doris was a member and so we as a family participated in various congregational events and programs. Many people in those days and since assumed that I was one of the pastors of the church.

Our children. . . . . All three of our children were born to us while in Bozeman during this period. And one died.

Doris and I wanted children and at first found that apparently we were not able to conceive. On one of our trips back to Illinois, we contacted The Cradle in Evanston, Illinois, which was a well-respected agency offering adoptions. We took the first step in applying to them. We returned to Montana and soon discovered thar a child was on the way. When we notified The Cradle they replied that this is often the result of merely applying to adopt. We were informed that the due date would be January 6.

On December 29, 1956 during a Christmas visit by my parents, we went for a ride up to West Yellowstone and that night after our return, signs of impending birth began to show up. On the morning of the 30th we took Doris to the hospital. As the birth process began that day and painful labor continued, it became evident to the attending physicians, Dr. Enebo and Dr. Sippel, that she would need to give birth by Caesarean Section, which then took place at 4:20 PM. Our first child was a boy, whom we named Ross William.

Almost two years later on October 27th 1958 our second child was born, also by Caesarean Section we named him Dan Peter. The Caesarean had been planned this time and in thinking through the pe-arranged date, Doris suggested October 25th, my birthday, which she thought would be nice. Dr. Sippel suggested that each person should have his own birthday and that he thought October 27th would be better. We accepted his idea and Dan was born on the 27th. (For which I have been glad.)

Sometime in early 1959, we became aware of Ross's kidney disease which some called Nephritis and others used the term Nephrosis. This confusion of terms indicates the unknown nature of his illness which was treated over the coming months, first in the Bozeman Deaconess

Hospital, then for five weeks at St. Mary's at the Mayo Clinic, and subsequently at Deaconess Hospital in Billings. All to no avail. He died at 7 PM at home on January 17, 1960. The saddest "epitaph" was Ross' own words: "Mommie, all the medicine is not making me better."

His funeral was conducted by our close fiend and pastor, Lad Anderson, in the sanctuary of First Presbyterian Church, Bozeman.. Clark Welch played the organ. I remember his playing "Be Still My Soul." He was laid to rest in Sunset Hills Cemetery in Bozeman. The two pall bearers were two young men from our campus ministry fellowship, Paul Biering and Sam Weeks.

On November 10, 1960, Rose Louise was born, the third and last of our children. While it would be unfair to consider Rose a replacement for Ross, she nevertheless brought joy to help us immensely during our time of sorrow.

Reflections on my experience in canpus ministry. . . . As I reflect on my eleven years in campus ministry, I see that period as quite pivotal. Seminary had given me anticipation for the parish ministry and prepared me well for my first call to the Yoder-Hawk Springs parish. It was a ministry within the church. In contrast, my ministry in Bozeman was within the academic institution, in which I was involved in trying, from a Christian perspective, to make a difference in the lives of students and other members of the academic community as well as in seeking to contribute to the overall effectiveness of the university itself. In preparation for this transformation in approach, the Association of Presbyterian University Pastors provided significant learning opportunities and experience through it annual national meetings and ongoing contact with other campus ministries regionally.

This re-orientation of the concept and approach in my Christian ministry prepared me significantly, I believe, for my part in the development of a new congregation with a new sense of direction and mission. In my third and final call, the development and continuing pastorate of St. Andrew Presbyterian Church in Billings. Most specifically, I now saw (1) my role as clergy in a local congregation as on an equal par with church members as an enabler rather than a ordained leader. I now understood my role as "equipping the saints for the work of ministry." And (2) the primary place and work of the church is to be in the world making a positive difference through expressing the love of God in Christ for all humankind through needful action in the world.

In the months leading up to the fall of 1967, the Presbytery of Yellowstone made the decision to organize a second Presbyterian congregation in Billings. Since 1959 the Presbytery had owned a 4.5 acre block on the west end of the city bounded by 24th Street West on the east and Cook Avenue on the north. Comity agreements among three mainline denominations in the Montana Council of Churches had designated that it was the Presbyterian Church's's turn to begin a second congregation, the Methodist and Congregational churches having done so by that time. The Session of First Presbyterian Church had been reluctant for a number of years until the Council of Churches urged the Presbytery to take action, a sort of "fish or cut bait" ultimatum. Thus in early 1966 the Presbytery of Yellowstone went ahead and began the process for the sdevelopment of a new congregation.

The First Church Session was invited to provide a steering Committee of thirteen couples to formulate plans for a new church. This did not necessarily imply that these folk would leave First Church to become members of the new congregation. This committee sought the guidance of the Board of National Missions. One of its first actions was to seek an organizing pastor in cooperation with the Ministerial Relations Committee of Yellowstone Presbytery, of which I was the Chairperson at the time. Subsequently I was called to be the organizing pastor.

Billings, Montana 1967-1992-founding pastor of St. Andrew Presbyterian Church in Billings, Montana, for the Presbytery of Yellowstone. We began our worship in Western Manor Nursing Home where we met for a number of years before developing our property. At first we used the basement of our house for after-school church school on Thursdays and various church meetings and activities, including my office and the office for a volunteer secretary. A few years later, we held our church school classes in Central Christian Church and then Mayflower United Church of Christ. In those years we used rented space across from Central Christian Church and later in Kimball Hall of Rocky Mountain College for our office.

From the earliest days of the steering committee which developed the plan for the new church two very formative convictions determined much of St. Andrew's style and thrust: (1) That we ought to be in ministry to the needs of the world outside ourselves. (2) That pastor and people in St. Andrew should be on an equal level and decisions and activities ought to have full participation of both members and pastor. These principles played a significant part as we developed our organization and activities.

In addition to St. Andrew duties, I served as pastoral counselor in a Pastoral Care Center located on the Rocky Mountain College campus, and as a part-time Extra Status Chaplain at Billings Deaconess Hospital in the late 1980s and early '90s. As an active member of the Presbytery, I served on the Christian Education and Ministerial Relations Committees at various times. I served as chair of each of these committees from time to time which placed me on Presbytery Council as well.. Synod responsibilities placed me on its Christian Education Committee and Synod Council as well at one time or another. I was elected Moderator of Presbytery for two different years and Moderator of the Synod of the Rockies once.

My outside involvements also included the Montana Association of Churches and the Yellowstone County Council of Churches. I served a term as President of each of these over the years.

As I review the twenty-five year period in my life in Billings, a number of memory paths emerge in my mind. Moving and getting established in Billings was in some ways our being given our part in the "American Dream." Fortunately when we were sill in Bozeman, we had invested in a small mutual fund of $2,500. Our contract with the Presbytery and then with St. Andrew church included a housing allowance instead of a manse. This, together with our mutual fund, enabled us to purchase a new three bedroom house on the corner of 29th St. West and Cook Avenue. (202 29th St. West), which became our home for the entire twenty-five years in Billings. And so our lives included the many delights and various responsibilities of home ownership over the

Billings years following. It always seemed to me that this provided us with a level of shared experience with our church members which made our understanding of our congregation more complete.

When we moved to Billings, Dan was in third grade and Rose in first. Each attended Meadowlark Elementary School, which was across 29th street from our house, enabling them to come home for lunch each day. Thus began very good experiences and achievements by each child throughout their public school days in Billings which included Will James Junior High and finally West High, each of which were within walking distance of our house. In all the years in which Dan and Rose were growing up, we almost always were together for daily family meals, and special celebration days were especially memorable.

As parents we were supportive and involved in the scouting program for both Dan and Rose. Beginning in Bozeman, Doris had been a Brownie leader and a Cub Scout Den mother and I had been a Cub Scout father. In Billings, Doris was a Girl Scout leader and I helped as a Boy Scout troop father. By his eighteenth birthday, Dan became an Eagle Scout.

While still in Bozeman, we had enrolled both Dan and Rose in an Orff method of early childhood music education experience taught by Ms. Carol Dietrich in her home. By the end of these classes, Carol got Dan started on the violin and Rose on the cello. In Billings, then, each took private lessons on their stringed instruments throughout their school days Each played in school orchestras throughout their school experiences. Their level of musical proficiency grew to the point that they each continued private lessons and participation in the Bozeman Symphony during their college years. Doris and I enjoyed immensely attending many orchestra concerts at all levels in which Dan and Rose played, including driving to Bozeman for symphony concerts there as well.

As a family we made yearly trips to Illinois to visit our parents: to LaSalle to visit Doris's parents and to Oak Park to visit my parents. We often drove, but sometimes took the North Coast Limited on the Northern Pacific RailRoad. Our parents also visited us. My parents drove or came by train yearly, Doris' not as frequently. Sometime in the early 1970s my parents moved from Oak Park to Bozeman where they entered Hillcrest retirement home and moved into a one- room apartment with all meals provided. As a family we frequently visited them there and often had a meal in the dining room with them. On February 18, 1969 Doris's mother died. (Louise Joop Schoening: (b.1/28/1890–d. 2/18.1969)) On May 21, 1976 Doris's father died (William Schoening (b. 2/1890-d. 5/21/1976). Both funerals were conducted at Trinity UCC Church in La Salle. Rev. Walter Kleffman, pastor at Trinity, conducted Doris' Mother's service. I conducted her father's service in place of Rev. Kleffman who was in the hospital at the time. In July 1980 my mother died (Louise Braun Krebill b. 5/24/1901-d. 7/ /1980) Her funeral was conducted by Rev. Margaret Balcom, interim pastor at Fisrt Presbyterian Church on Bozeman. On October 17, 1985 my father died (Armin P. Krebill b.9/29/1898-d.10/17/1985) His funeral was conducted by Rev. Tyra Talley, interim pastor at First Presbyterian in Bozeman.

St. Andrews, Scotland

In July of 1970 I had the privilege of attending a Theological Institute at the University of St. Andrews in St Andrews, Scotland. This was on the invitation of my friend, Lad Anderson, then pastor of First Presbyterian Church in Great Falls, Montana. In appreciation for my work with Montana Presbyterian Students in Bozeman, the Session of the Great Falls First Church paid for my trip. I accompanied Lad on this three-week experience.

At the conclusion of this event, Doris, Dan, and Rose met me in London where we rented a camper van and we spent two weeks traveling in England, Scotland, France, Germany, Holland, and Belgium.

Drummond, New Zealand

During June, July, and August 1987 I served as Interim Pastor of the Oreti Parish in Drummond and Oreti, Southland, in New Zealand. Our friend, Jack Wells, had served this parish after his retirement from the Presbyterian Church in Pocatello, Idaho. He suggested that I come to the Oreti Parish while he took my place at St. Andrew for three months. This was agreed upon by both the Oreti Parish and St. Andrew. We flew to Los Angeles and flew from LAX on a night flight to New Zealand on Air New Zealand landing in Christchurch. And then after a few hours visit to the Square we boarded a flight to Invercargill. The next three months were a wonderfully memorable experience for us. My ministerial service was much he same as my work earlier in Wyoming with two congregations. We were provided with a car and given a day off each week and a week of vacation. This enabled us to tour much of the South Island.

PART 6

RETIREMENT

I retired when I turned 65, on October 25, 1992, and we moved to a house we had purchased at 3414 Wagon Wheel Road, in Bozeman, Montana. The house was a single story three bedroom "rancher" located on a well-developed half-acre lot with five very large spruce trees, three apple trees, as well as a small plum tree and an abundance of shrubbery including a number of lilac bushes, maples, and aspens. We cultivated the large garden plot which was partially surrounded by lots of raspberry bushes. We enjoyed our yard immensely in every season and kept bird feeders and a bird bath throughout the year. Through the winter a number of white tailed deer visited our yard as well as an occasional skunk. In the fall, black bear came looking for food for their winter consumption before hibernating. On one occasion a mother bear and two cubs visited our yard and ate bird food and apples on the ground. She then urged her cubs up a tree in our yard next to a neighbor's shed. She then climbed up on the shed and went to sleep for the rest of the afternoon.

In February of 2012, we moved into Aspen Pointe, a Hillcrest Retirement facility apartment at 1201 Highland Blvd, Apt. B-209, Bozeman, MT, in order to reduce our indoor and outdoor home and yard care. We found that living in a second floor two-bedroom apartment with weekly maid service and a meal a day provided and an underground garage accessible via two elevators to be too "institutional" and confining for us.

At the end of July 2013, we moved from Aspen Pointe, a Bozeman Lodge cottage at 1419A N. Hunters Way, Bozeman, Montana, which we found more to our liking. In many ways this was like returning to our own house in which we prepared all our own meals and had an attached garage. In terms of the social context the cottage was much more private, since we did not take our meals in the Lodge nor attend the various programs available there.

In the spring of 2019 we moved over to an apartment in Bozeman Lodge to obtain a greater amount of emergency care in case of accident or sickness. At ages 93 and 91 this made sense.

However we do miss our home on Wagon Wheel of twenty years and especially mourn the loss of our yard and the large deck which looked out over the backyard. This is the one down side of retirement for us.

As I contemplate the meaning of retirement, it comes to me that retirement involves the turning over to others a significant amount of one's active engagements. I no longer have responsibility for St. Andrew Church. Since leaving I have often said to myself, *I had my turn, now that belongs to someone else.*

Now Dan and Rose and their families have in some sense taken Doris's and my place. It is their turn now. We are the onlookers as they raise their children and enjoy their achievements and activities in which their children are involved. We are exceedingly fortunate that we can be very proud onlookers as we observe the successes of Dan and Jody, Rose and Tim, and of their children. It gives us great joy to exult in their happiness and achievements.

In the very first years of retirement, I volunteered at a number of tasks: I did some pastoral work for Hospice, served on the Rockhaven Camp committee and the library committee at Church, and did a bit of supply preaching. But now I have happily given up these jobs. Soon after retiring I began reading novels and in time, began writing novels, which I have enjoyed immensely.

Retirement has given Doris and me the opportunity to take day trips together, such as drives through Yellowstone, as well as visits to Rose and Tim and their family in Idaho.

A most enjoyable and satisfying activity in retirement has been fiction writing. It was only after retirement that I took the first hesitant step into the writing of a novel. Earlier, while in the ministry there was a slight glimmering of a scene for a story, but I did nothing about this thought, except to mention it briefly to Doris.

Writing for publication. . . . After we retired Doris encouraged me to start trying to write "my novel." I had no confidence that anyone would want to read my story, much less publish it, but she encouraged me to start anyway.

The scene which had captivated me was one in which I had participated on many occasions during the grave-side services which I conducted at the local cemetery. Something about the emotion of these moments among the family members frequently stimulated my imagination and eventually became the seed for my first book, *A Place Called Fairhavens,* which begins with the scene at the cemetery. With little or no anticipation of what the course this story would take, I let the characters in the opening scene begin to "live." After the story ended some 300 pages later, I found myself sad to leave "Max" and "Bronwyn." This impelled me to begin another story, this time with entirely different characters in a different Montana location. But, again, the story grew from an opening seed, which in this case was a scene I had photographed many years earlier of an abandoned gold mining camp, which brought *Harry's Legacy* to life. Without prior planning the story once again unfolded as I went along. That was in 2001. Now nine more novels have come about in somewhat the same way.

At the suggestion of a few members of St. Andrew Church in Billings in 2004 I published many of the monthly devotional readings I had written for Andrews's Net, the St. Andrew newsletter, in the form of a year-long daily devotional book, which I named *Words for Thinking and Thoughts for Meditation,*

In 2007, in collaboration with Doris and our granddaughter, Martha, I wrote and published *The Cowboy Bob Treasury–A Children's Read-Aloud Book.* At the urging of my family, I put together a collection of "Cowboy Bob" bed time stories which I had made up to tell to our children and grandchildren. Ten-year-old Martha did the illustrations assisted by Doris.

Finally, I highly recommend retirement to those who don't seem to want to quit!

Throughout the year what were some of the happy days?

- playing in the back yard in the snow with Ricky.
- setting up a village in the entire spare bedroom on Marion street.
- going to a soda fountain with John Jones for Green Rivers and talk.
- leaning over the checkroom door on a busy Saturday night.
- walking with Doris on Sunday afternoons in the flower garden of Wilder Park.
- sitting with Doris in her backyard in LaSalle late on a summer night.
- walking into the New Gatlinburg Inn on our honeymoon.
- being driven over the Smoky Mountains in a Buick convertible.
- enjoying a first supper made by Doris in our apartment in McCormick Hall.
- eating Sunday dinner in a Morgan Park family home.
- driving with Doris to Scottsbluff and eating in the Chinese restaurant.
- seeing Bozeman for the first time covered with lots of snow & the ski shop on Olive.
- coming back to the Townhouse for breakfast with Doris after a Danforth Chapel service.
- pulling our kids on a sled along paths in the snow in our yard on Cleveland.

- spending Sunday afternoons with Bassetts and Locks in one of their yards.
- sitting in the sun at Zephyr Point on Lake Tahoe.
- Walking Porcupine Trail in the evening with Doris, Dan and Rose at Zephyr Point.
- driving home on Broadwater on a Saturday afternoon.
- celebrating Christmas with Dan and Rose and Doris in our 29th St. living room.
- going in the Abbey on Iona with Lad Anderson.
- driving along the country roads in Scotland with Doris, Dan and Rose in the caravan.
- driving into Invercargill, New Zealand with Doris.
- stopping at Cape Reinga on the North Island of New Zealand with Doris.
- Walking out to the mail box and looking at the Bridgers beyond Wagon Wheel Road.

PART 7

LIFE EVERLASTING AFTER DEATH

I believe there will be life everlasting after death. But it is beyond human, earthbound words and thought forms. Metaphors are used instead which very well may point to truth, but cannot betaken as literal descriptions. Jesus used the metaphor of "many mansions in the Father's house. The Apostle Paul spoke of "then seeing face to face" after only "seeing in a mirror dimly." For me, the most insightful and hope-filled look ahead is the statement by John in Revelation. "See, the home of God is with mortals. He will dwell with them; they will be his peoples, and God himself will be with them; he will wipe every tear from their eyes. Death will be no more; mourning and crying and pain will be no more, for the first things have passed away." (Revelation 21:3,4)

Whatever has been good and beautiful this side of the grave will be, I believe, good and beautiful beyond our ability to imagine. Whatever here has been negative in any way will simply not be any longer present. All that hurt or destroyed happiness will be gone forever. Sorrow for our losses here will be replaced with infinite joy. Death will be replaced with infinite life. Thus, loved ones lost will be with us in a way we cannot even begin to imagine.

And most of all we will be with God without any separation.

APPENDIX

Books I have published through Xlibris

Novels:

A PLACE CALLED FAIRHAVENS - A Novel. By curious coincidence the fortunes of a Montana resort and a bed & breakfast in New Zealand become intertwined, dramatically affecting the lives of two people a world apart: a young pastor who flees to New Zealand after losing his congregation and his wife, and a young woman who owns an inn on the south shore of New Zealand.

2001 (ISBN: 0-7388-5122-1 312 pages)

HARRY'S LEGACY -A novel set in Montana and New Zealand. For over a century the ruins of a gold mine in the mountains of western Montana held the secrets of the two men who owned and operated the mine. When the ghostly remains of this gold mining development are discovered by Tom and Heather while cross country skiing, its story begins to unravel. Forgotten injustices are discovered, as Tom and Heather discover each other as well, as they make amends for former wrongs.

2001 (ISBN: 1-4010-275-X 227 pages)

HERITAGE HIDDEN -A Novel. A university professor in mortal fear for his life has fled to Montana. His life becomes intertwined with that of a local inkeeper who befriends him despite the suspicions of neighboring townsfolk. In a mysterious timewarp, his past connects with that of a visiting piano soloist, which leads to a future in which life-threatening dangers are resolved and new relationships are deepened.

2002 (ISBN: 1-4010-6383-7 236 pages)

MORIAH'S VALLEY A place of healing in a time of mourning. A novel set in the Boulder Valley south of Big Timber, Montana. A social researcher comes to Montana to study population changes and their effect upon the lives of the residents of a small town who mourn the loss of family and friends who have moved away. He falls in love with the town, and in particular with a young woman who helps him resolve his own grief.

2003 (ISBN: 1-4134-1537-7 - 340 pages)

WESTBOUND -A Novel. The magic of the West captures the imagination of a young man from Chicago and entices him to spend his life on the plains of Montana. Becoming the pastor of a small congregation near Miles City, Montana, he finds geographical and cultural differences both intriguing and frustrating. His choice of the ministry was too disturbing for his fiancé, who broke their engagement before he entered seminary. He begins his ministry as a single person, but not for long! But that is not the end of the story.

2006 (ISBN: 1-4257-1631-8 - 396 pages)

SYLVA -A Montana-based novel, this time set along the Musselshell in Wheatland County. A young woman who grew up in a rigid sect in Indiana escapes when she is abducted by a man claiming to be her uncle. He forces her to go with him across the country on his way to Idaho. She breaks loose when he stops for gas on highway No. 12 in central Montana. Thus begins her astounding life of freedom in the imaginary town of Harrington.

2009 (ISBN: 978-1-4363-8937 185 pages

RETURN TO ARROW RIVER A novel. Andrew McEwan had left his house on the Arrow River of New Zealand in the 1880's to seek his fortune in the gold fields of Montana. Now his great grandson has come to Montana from New Zealand to trace the story of Andrew McEwan, who, having fled from Montana in fear of his life, had entered upon a long and perilous journey to return to New Zealand. While a sequel to both FAIRHAVENS and HARRY'S LEGACY, this is a complete story on its own and can be enjoyed without having read the first two novels.

2010 (ISBN: 978-1-4535-2690-3 146 pages

U-TURN Two young friends in love separate unhappily after high school graduation. One to pursue his dream of wealth and prestige as he seeks the glitter of big city America. The other to remain in her beloved hometown on the banks of the Yellowstone River in southern Montana. Almost a lifetime later, the struggles and twists in their life journeys eventually bring about a conergence of their two pathwys.

2012 (ISBN: 978-1-4771-2861-9 166 pages)

TRAILS' END From the banks of the Mississippi and from the shores of the Mediterranean to the Chicago of Al Capone they came: Landino from his native Italy and Eleanor from her home in Iowa. Each had been drawn to the glamor of the city. Instead they had fallen prey to the influence of the Capone mob as it was spreading its criminal activities throughout Chicago. After escaping from Capone's grip, Landino and Eleanor meet in a gold mining town in Montana. But the tentacles of Big Al persist as the two try to carve out a new life for themselves in Montana.

2014 (ISBN: 978-1-4990-3721-0 212 pages)

MR. SWENSEN Very little was known of the personal life of Mr. Swensen, professor of history in a small Midwestern college. Apparently a bachelor, he lived alone on the third floor of one of the buildings on campus and took most of his meals in the dining hall, usually sitting alone. While his courses were popular among students, his personal life remained a mystery. He had been born Karl Erickson in Reese Creek, Montana, a heritage he himself had been unaware of until later in his reclusive life. In a surprising yet bittersweet turn of events, he finds love and discovers his own origins. As result, his career expands in a way he had never before imagined. And yet his personal life continues to be a mystery to others, but will be revealed to the reader!

2016 (ISBN 978-1-5144-8750-1 136 pages)

THE PROMISE Growing up in early nineteenth century Germany, Heinrich and Amanda were joined by the promise they made to marry each other one day in the future. But they were forced apart when their families emigrated separately to America at different times. After many futile attempts to find each other in the new world in which they now lived, each reluctantly has to settle into a new life separated from their promised one, until years later when their lives converge in a most surprising set of circumstances. Is it too late for their promise to be kept? Perhaps.

2018 (978-1-9845-6617-5 107 pages)

My view & standards for my own fiction writing:

The **story** ought to be believable and true to life even though it is a figment of my imagination. The **setting** should be, for the most part, actual places surrounding the imagined location in which the story takes plaçe. All my novels have a setting somewhere in Montana. The **characters** will be imaginary people, the depiction of whose lives, however, is true to life. Most of the people in the story should be folks I would like to know and hopefully, with whom the reader will also enjoy associating. The underlying **attitudes, values, and behavior** of the leading characters will develop out of what I interpret as the Christian worldview and theological understanding of the human condition.

Devotional Book

WORDS FOR THINKING AND THOUGHTS FOR MEDITATION

—366 Daily Devotionals A resource for private devotions or for prayer and Bible study groups in which life concerns are considered in the light of God's message to us. Scripture, comment and prayer for each day of the year help to deepen personal, family, or group experience of Christ for daily life.

2004 (ISBN: 1-4134-5206-X - 432 pages)

Children's Book

THE COWBOY BOB TREASURY - Read-Aloud Stories for Children. Originally these were bedtime stories told in the family for a couple of generations. Illustrated by Martha Krebill with the assistance of Doris Krebill

2007 (ISBN: 978-14257-8223-8 35 pages)\

A FINAL MUSING

And now in the waning days of autumn, a few more words. I am deeply thankful to others in my family for their assistance in bringing to fruition AUTUMN REFLECTIONS: to my daughter, Rose whose painting is on the cover; to my son, Dan for technical assistance and for the photos on the front and back covers, for the expert editing by Jody, my daughter-in-law; for my wife, Doris's encouragement and patience. I thank my long time friend, John Schroeder, and distant relative, Olga Hirschler, for family history information, and I offer my appreciation to the many friends and family members whose lives have touched mind and appear in these pages! And finally I thank Kevin Laguno and others at Xlibris for their patient assistance in bringing my life and times into print!